# Mercy in the Wilderness

SUSIE M. LARSON

Foreword by Terri Blackstock

PUBLISHING

Belleville, Ontario, Canada

# MERCY IN THE WILDERNESS
## Copyright © 2000, Susie Larson

All Scripture quotations, unless otherwise specified, are from the *Holy Bible*, New Living Translation. (Copyright @ 1996. Used by permission of Tyndale House Publishers, Inc., Wheaton, Illinois 60189. All rights reserved.)

Scriptures marked NIV are from the *New International Version* of the Bible. (Copyright © 1973, 1978, 1984 International Bible Society. Used by permission of Zondervan Bible Publishers. All rights reserved.)

## ISBN: 1-55306-147-0

*First Printing, September 2000*
*Second Printing, August 2002*

*Essence Publishing* is a Christian Book Publisher dedicated to furthering the work of Christ through the written word. For more information, contact: 44 Moira Street West, Belleville, Ontario, Canada K8P 1S3. Phone: 1-800-238-6376. Fax: (613) 962-3055. E-mail: info@essencegroup.com Internet: www.essencegroup.com

Printed in Canada
by

*Essence*
PUBLISHING

*This book is lovingly dedicated to Jesus Christ,*
*who truly makes all things new.*

# Table of Contents

# ACKNOWLEDGMENTS

hanks to Essence Publishing for your hard work and wonderful support. Bless you. Thanks to Patty Fischer for planting the seed when we were in college. Love you. A special thanks to Terri Blackstock for encouraging me to finish the book, you are an inspiration. Thanks to Barbi Franklin for your kindness and powerful words at a time when I needed them. Thanks to Del and Darrold for the seed that is still hanging on my wall. You never let me give up. Bless you for that. Thanks to Joyce, Sandy, Pam and Allyse for the great cover ideas. (Joyce, thanks for your extra time.) To Charitie Shively, one of the coolest teens I know, your gift blew me away. You are marked by God to do amazing things. Don't ever forget that. To Daryl and Digger Jackson for backing this project in the most humble, generous way possible. May your love and support be returned tenfold!

To my parents for their precious love, I love you back. To my siblings and their families; Gary, Greg, Pam, Jeff, Karen and Krissy. Thanks for the memories and for loving me just as I am. To the Larson family, thank you for your love and acceptance. Thank you most of all for giving me Kevin, my love and companion. Daryl, you will always be my forever friend. To my mentors, Darrold and Del, bless you for pointing me to Jesus. To my friend, Katie, for taking some of my home school duties so I could finish this book, thank you. To my Cracker Barrel girlfriends, Betsy, Joyce and Therese—I love you! Mary Jo, you are a soul mate to me. Bless you for always being there. I love you, too, Michael! I thank You, Lord, for our prayer group: Dan and Sandy, Annie and Luke, Pam and Scott. Our times together have driven me deeper in my faith walk. There is no turning back. I love you all so much! To the people and staff of Bridgewood Community Church, may we forever be doing what God is blessing! Love you. To Mike Brown at Life Time Fitness, thanks for challenging me right out the door! Remember your first love like you told me to. To Dee Ann for showing up at my door on the worst days, you always knew what I needed. I love you. To my three young men, Jake, Luke and Jordan—may you always go after the heart of God and never let up. I love you more than life and I always will. To my husband and forever friend, Kevin, you could have left when things seemed impossible, but you never did. You not only stayed, but you carried us to the cross, time and time again. You are my love. Finally, to Jesus of Nazareth for saving my soul once and for all, and for restoring my heart over and over again. I will follow You forever. I love You most.

# FOREWORD

few years ago I received a letter from a reader named Susie Larson, and with it came a tape of a workshop she had done. She told me in the letter that she enjoyed my books and the ministry value of them, and wanted to share her ministry with me.

Her letter came at a time when I was suffering some trials—not terrible ones, but the kind that occupy your mind and spirit when you could or should be doing other things. I remember popping the tape into the cassette player, and lying down to listen. I heard of the trials she had suffered for so many years in her young family's life, and the hope and message of those tapes gave me the perspective I needed in facing my own trials.

I learned from those tapes that, sometimes, the crisis can be the blessing. I learned that God wants us to love

Him with our heart, soul, mind and strength, even when He isn't giving us what we want. I learned that the gift of His Son on the cross was more than enough, even if He never answers another of our prayers.

But He always does answer. Sometimes we're just too near-sighted to see how.

Susie's tape was one of God's instruments in teaching me this important lesson. I've since used the concept in many of my novels, and have received letters from many readers who have been touched by it, as well. Because I think God's people need to hear this in as many ways as possible, I encouraged Susie to write it in a book. I knew I needed to see it written down, so I could refer back to it again and again, and I hoped others could share in this wonderful truth, as well.

I hope this message of God's divine perspective will touch you as it touched me. I pray that it will guide you through whatever trial you encounter, and give you great comfort as you keep your eyes on Him.

Terri Blackstock
Author of *Word of Honor and Seasons Under Heaven*

# INTRODUCTION

Do you ever feel that God is so far away, He couldn't possibly know that your heart is breaking? Have you cried out to Him to find the response you hear is the echo in your soul? How do we survive these trying times and where is God when we feel so alone? Is He out there, and does He care? Or are we left to figure things out by ourselves?

I have asked myself these questions and many more like them. The truth of the matter is that God is so very near to the brokenhearted and is watching us more closely than we can imagine. He is on His throne and has not for a minute stopped being the One who is intimately acquainted with our sorrows and our joys. He never promised us a path free of debris. He did guarantee the grace to see us through the messes that life promises.

There is such a precious sweetness in finding another willing to walk with us through the storm.

God is not only willing to walk with us through the battles of this life, He knows the way out and is patient enough to move at our pace. He is the only One who can take the ashes from our war and mold them into jewels fit for a crown. He asks for our trust when He says, "Take a left," and we think we should go right. He patiently waits for us to hand Him our trust so He can show us His faithfulness. Many say that life isn't fair and it really isn't. When you compare what the Lord asks and what He gives us, you'll find that they are worlds apart.

This book is for the heart that longs to see God. He is here right now. Take a journey with me and look for the countless ways He has shown up in our lives. May it encourage you to know that when you look for Him with all of your heart, He will be found by you.

May the Lord bless you as you read.

*Susie Larson*

*But whatever happens ...*
*You must live in a manner worthy of the Good News about Christ, as citizens of heaven. Then, whether I come and see you again or only hear about you, I will know that you are standing side by side, fighting together for the Good News. Don't be intimidated by your enemies. This will be a sign to them that they are going to be destroyed, but that you are going to be saved, even by God himself. For you have been given not only the privilege of trusting in Christ but also the privilege of suffering for him.*
*We are in this fight together.*

Philippians 1:27-30

## CHAPTER ONE

# A Brief Stop

I wondered if bringing my boys to this place was a good idea. They were so curious about where their dad had to stop in the middle of the day, but did they really need to actually visit the place? They wondered what exactly made him so sick, so tired and so unhealthy looking and it seemed the right thing to show them.

Now that I am here with them at my side, I find that there's a knot in my stomach. They appear more interested than stressed. When Kevin walked in, he was surprised to see us waiting for him. He managed a smile as he sat next to us in the waiting room. He had determined to work a couple of hours that morning. I wondered if he had gotten any flak for not wearing a tie. I wondered when he would get the color back in his face.

We chatted as the kids climbed all over him. I can't believe I forgot to comb Luke's hair. His hair was jacked up on one side. Jordan was walking on his tiptoes again. "Jordan, on your feet, honey. Please don't eat so many cookies, they're for the other patients too. Come and sit down. Pick a chair and go with it." I wondered if I should apologize to the other patients in the waiting room.

They were old enough to be grandparents. They seemed to empathize. Thankfully, Jake sat quietly and looked at a magazine. "Kevin," the receptionist called, "they are ready for you." Kevin really liked her. She had become a "mother" to all the patients who daily graced her with their presence.

We walked back together and met all the nurses who had become Kevin's friends. They brought us into a very sterile room that had a bed surrounded by an enormous machine. Is this what "clean" smells like? Definitely nothing could grow in this environment. The floor was lined with odd shaped, lead blocks that each had a plastic shield on them. "This one is your daddy's," the nurse said to my boys. "It was designed just for him. The big, lead block protects the area that we don't want to hit, and the open area shows us where he needs radiation."

As they listened intently to this amazing information, I found myself glancing across the hall. There was the room we first visited several weeks before. We made it through the major surgery to remove the cancer, but the scan showed that the tumor had tentacles. He would need a higher level of radiation than we had originally thought.

I looked over and saw myself in that room again. Kevin seemed like a little boy that day. He had to lie on the very narrow bed as still as possible. He couldn't move because they were mapping him. This is a process where they shine laser beams on his midsection to determine where to radiate.

There were several nurses hustling back and forth between drawing on his stomach and chest and operating their machines. When they would find a certain spot, they would inject a small needle under the skin and give him a permanent tattoo. He had a small towel covering his genitals. Sometimes the nurses were in such a hurry they would only partially cover him back up again, but he was not to move an inch. I stood at the head of his bed with my hands on his cheeks. He stared right past me to the ceiling. I kept telling him that I loved him and was so sorry that he had to go through this. Little tears would escape him and trickle down the sides of his face. My vulnerable love. That's what I called him that day. He had always been the strength that Jesus used to hold our family together. He shouldered much stress and remained kind and loving through it all. Now it was he who needed our shoulders, our kindness and our strength.

He proposed to me under a starry night. He washed my feet as a symbol of his heart to love and serve me as his forever companion. We prayed right then and there that our love, our life would not be one of "playing church"or working hard to present well, but one of authenticity and faith. We wanted our children to see us hanging onto God in a real and daily way. We wanted to demonstrate our faith before them by bringing the Lord into everything, not just some things. This was our passion and our heart's cry. The worst thing, we thought, would be for them to know Jesus and become apathetic about Him.

Looking back, I found myself amazed that what I had hoped for our family was very similar to what we were experiencing. And yet, the getting there was a far cry from where I ever wanted to go. I longed for a family that was real, authentic and in love with Jesus. I wanted us to care about the things that mattered most. I didn't want to be just another self-indulgent family whose deepest concern would be when they would make their next big purchase. Little did I know that our road to humility and authenticity was a long one.

CHAPTER TWO

# *Critical or Thankful?*

amily. What comes to your mind when you hear that word? God had a beautiful plan when He designed the family. I believe He created the family to be a representation of how He wanted the church to operate. Over and over in Scripture we are exhorted to love one another and bear with another's weakness. So many verses challenge us to think on what is good and right, and pray for what is weak and wrong. Unfortunately, our rights and personal comforts tend to take a front seat to love and sacrifice. We fall into the rut of fault-finding and come up empty-handed. Oh that we could tap into the power of the Almighty and take hold of the love that covers a multitude of sins! What a blessing it is when family members can be there for each other during times of struggle as well as celebration!

Unfortunately, this picture seems to be the exception rather than the rule. For many, the family represents a place of insecurity and painful memories. Hard times hit, relationships unravel and many are left disillusioned. Why does this happen so often? Is it because we look for the journey to be painless and for people to be perfect? It is so tempting to look to the tangible things in life to come through for us and tell us what we want to hear. When our "messengers" don't deliver, we feel justified in blaming and discarding them in search of another situation or relationship that will feed our ego and leave our soul hungry.

What are we to do with disappointments? People can be hurtful and this can cause us to walk with a limp for some time. When others disappoint us, how do we walk in a way that would please God? Is it possible that the person or circumstance didn't really fail us at all, but rather our expectations were misplaced? Even so, people do fail us and hurt us miserably. Is God big enough to make something beautiful of it?

This is one of life's lessons I had to learn the hard way. In the mid to late '80s, there was unleashed a recovery movement in the church at large. Many were looking into their pasts to figure out their present. Much healing took place during this time. For the first time the wounded were able to speak out loud of the abuse they endured and find healing for their pain. It became a time of "shaking the rugs" and looking at everything we had swept under there. Rivers of tears flowed from the relief of bringing to light that which was buried before it was dead. It was awesome to see countless people set free from what bound them as they learned to speak the truth in love.

And yet as with any movement, extremes were taken to the point of destruction. Confrontations were happening everywhere and relationships were blowing up. The pendulum seemed to swing so far to the right that things were getting analyzed to death. Once again, something that was meant for good, when taken too far, became a curse. People divided over petty issues as they pounced on every imperfection that arose in their relationships.

I was one of those people who over-analyzed my childhood. I took all the information that was available in the present day and matched it against the way my father parented me. I wanted him not to care so much about how things "looked." I wanted him to talk more about his feelings. When he wanted me to be careful about how much of myself I should share with another, I interpreted it as an effort to quench who I really was. He spoke one language, I spoke another.

In the beginning of November 1987, my father discovered quite a bit of blood in his urine. He was told he most likely had cancer and kept it a secret for several months. He did not want to disrupt the holidays for his family so he waited to do something about it. On January 2, he sat my mom down and then shared with the rest of us this thing he had kept inside. A couple months later, he was scheduled for surgery.

As I looked around the waiting room at my whole family, I noticed how very different we all were. We were joined together because we came from the same parents. The bond we shared was deep because of the work my parents put into keeping us together. It took us a few years, but we really learned how to celebrate our differences and build on the things that mattered most. We sipped on coffee, and caught up on each other's lives. Although the circumstances were stressful, we were glad to be together.

It wasn't long before the surgeon came out to talk to us. He led us to the patient conference room and asked us to sit down. None of us felt much like sitting. The tumor was definitely malignant. My mom's knees buckled right under her. My brothers held her up. The sisters and I hugged each other and choked back the tears in an effort to be strong for our mom. My dad had his tumor removed and was sent home after a few days. A couple months later, he was to go in for a follow-up exam.

The night before this appointment, as I was praying, I sensed the Lord telling me to go with my parents for this checkup. I called my mom. She replied, "Oh honey, that's so sweet, but you really don't need to. This is just an out-patient appointment and it's really no big deal." It didn't take her long to realize I wasn't "asking" if I could go with them. She asked me to join them for lunch afterwards. I had a feeling that there would be no lunch that day.

The test was scheduled to last forty-five minutes. We sat there for one hour, then two, then three.... I watched my mom shift in her seat as her uneasiness grew. We held hands, prayed and waited. She could not have gone through this day alone. Our name was called and the surgeon was ready to talk to us. The look on his face spoke volumes. The first tumor they removed was a grade level of one plus. In this short time, he had grown several more tumors, which were graded at four plus, obviously more serious. The doctor had also expressed concern because the whole lining of his bladder was looking diseased.

## Critical or Thankful?

My mom wilted in my arms and sobbed. I prayed. I felt sick to my stomach because I knew that my relationship with my father left much to be desired. I was so close to my mom and my siblings, but I felt that my dad and I were miles apart. Why did he have to be sick now? After comforting my mom, I went to update the rest of the family. Everyone was shocked and quite rattled. My dad was to go home and recover from this surgery. I don't quite remember how many days we had to wait to find out where else the cancer had gone, but it seemed like an eternity. We knew for sure that he would need more surgery. The worst case scenario wasn't something we were ready to talk about.

My parents had two huge priorities as far as our family was concerned. They were Christmas and summer vacation. It meant everything (and cost everything) for them to make memories for us. Every summer we would go to the same resort far up north in Minnesota. We would have a blast together. This year would have to be different. We knew going to the resort was not an option. We wondered if it would ever be again. My dad needed to have his family around him before he faced whatever lay ahead.

My brother hosted an early Fourth of July picnic at his house. All seven kids, their spouses and a dozen grandchildren gathered for a great time. There was this underlying ache in our hearts, but maybe that made our time together more sweet. The kids blew bubbles, played in the sand and ran around the yard. Some of the adults engaged in a heated battle of horseshoes. A few others reclined on the deck and soaked in the sunny day. This is where we all needed to be, and this is where my dad belonged.

After a long and perfect day, my parents headed home. My mom put the leftovers in the fridge and changed her clothes. She noticed Dad was nowhere in the house. She found him sitting out on their deck in deep thought. She went out to sit with him in his silence. She knew what he was thinking but waited for him to be ready to tell her. Together they cried for all they had, and all they might lose. They held each other and hung on for dear life.

The days that followed were filled with a groaning too deep for words. My dad lay in the intensive care unit looking barely alive. He had one dim light on in his room which gave a gray tint to his skin. He had a thick tube coming out of his nose that looked miserably uncomfortable. The countless other tubes came from his midsection. A few tubes had clear liquid, others were filled with blood. The different gadgets spit out sounds that seemed to be in sync with each other.

I could tell that my dad was in so much pain even though he didn't move a muscle nor utter a word. He lay there with eyes closed and his mouth partially opened. If it weren't for the steady rise and fall of his chest, I would have thought he was dead. They had removed his bladder, his prostate, his appendix and a small portion of his intestine. As I sat by his hospital bed watching him sleep, my mom told me stories of his growing-up days. I don't know if this was the first time these things had been told to me, or if this was just the first time that I actually heard them.

My dad grew up with a father who drank too much. He and his four sisters lived in poverty and were many times left to fend for themselves. There were times when my dad and his sisters' home was their car. That's where they would meet at the end of the day and that's where they would sleep at night. I tried to imagine what that was like, but I just couldn't. While other children were going home to dinner on the stove and a warm bed to sleep in, he and his sisters retreated to the emptiness of a car. My heart began to absolutely break as I heard these and other stories about my dad's life.

My dad had made something of himself. He married the love of his life and they had seven children together. He moved his family into a nice home and built a life for us there. He did not want us to see what he had seen as a child. He became the mayor of the city we lived in and served in that capacity for twenty-seven years.

My mom went to get some coffee and left me alone at my father's bedside. He was asleep in spite of the irritation of tubes and noisy machines. I stared at him and felt broken and ashamed. God spoke to me at that moment and said, "Susie, I am well aware of the fact that you think your father did not understand you the way you thought he should. But the deepest truth is that he loved you with his life. He knew what he had seen as a child was not for your eyes. He worked tirelessly to build a life for you far from what he knew. You measure his love and understanding against the overabundance of information that is now out there. I measure his love by the motive in his heart. He looked at what he lacked and worked so hard to make sure that you wouldn't. That, my dear, is love in the purist sense. I am less concerned with 'the way' he loves than I am with a heart that doesn't see that as love. You have much to learn from this man. He deserves your utmost love and respect."

I laid my head on his bed, I grabbed fistfuls of his blankets and I wept. I apologized to him and I apologized to God. How could I be so short-sighted? I had somehow gotten lost in the psychoanalysis of things. I missed the bigger picture. I found that I was looking at the flaws with a magnifying glass and letting that be the defining factor of our relationship. I soon realized that the flaws are there in any relationship. We have to ask ourselves if we are mulling over these flaws to the point of destruction, or placing them in proper perspective with the preciousness of that person? There is obviously a place for analyzing issues, and that is to bring understanding. The purpose then is for that understanding to bring us to a deeper place with God and an increased capacity to love His people. How easy it is to notice the speck in another's eye and miss the log in our own. We have our own wretched flaws. There is enough in each of us to single-handedly send Christ to the cross. We need to give grace and we need to receive it.

As I lay there and grieved over my self-centeredness, my mind raced back over some of the good memories of my childhood. On the weekends, my parents would move the furniture out of the living room and teach us how to jitterbug. They were excellent dancers and they had fun teaching us what they knew. We actually became pretty good!

I then remembered cuddling next to my dad as he told me how important it was to keep myself pure until marriage. He would tell me how I just couldn't give away a gift that was meant only for my husband. He said, "Honey, picture yourself coming back to your high school reunion, holding onto your husband's arm. Are you two holding your heads high because you saved yourselves for each other, or are you ashamed because there are other boys in that room who have known you in a way they shouldn't have?" That never left me.

My life has been nothing like my dad's had been. My mom and dad had made sure of that. As I have learned to look at myself, I have learned a lot of hard lessons. I am afraid that my generation may be the most selfish one yet. We tend to think the universe truly rotates on an axis with our name on it. It seems that we will hold others to a standard that we wouldn't even think of upholding ourselves. We can't believe it when someone offends or hurts us, but we are unwilling to sit and listen to the impact that our actions have had on others.

Love is patient, kind and "others" oriented. It keeps no account of wrongs and rejoices when another succeeds. Have we given our parents the grace that we will need when we are in their place? I have learned that the only way psycho-analysis will bring us to a better place is if it is coupled with love and grace. Without these two elements, it becomes a load of arrogant noise that focuses on the shortcomings of others, while missing the artwork Christ performed when He created them. Are their relationships in your life that are broken for petty reasons? Don't waste any more time! As far as it concerns you, offer love, forgiveness and grace. Others may or may not respond favorably. But your actions will make a difference in the whole scheme of things.

My parents have loved me through it all—from being a child dependent on them for survival, to being a teen who knew everything, to being an adult who now humbly understands all they gave up for me. Bless you, Mom and Dad.

CHAPTER THREE

# *White Knuckles and Aching Hearts*

ou are going to bed for three months." I listened to my doctor's orders wondering how in the world I could go to bed for three days let alone three months. At six months along, the stresses of life and a weak cervix caused me to go into labor early. I required surgery and countless trips to the hospital to keep the baby inside of me. The medicine I was prescribed made me feel restless and shaky. I had a fifteen-month-old whom I tried to parent from the couch on the days when no one else could take him.

Delivery came three weeks early. The doctor on call burst through the door and spouted, "Roll over onto your back, I have to get this needle in your stomach."

Taken back a bit I asked, "Can I wait until this contraction is over, I am having severe back labor?"

"It's not going to kill you to roll four inches onto your back!" His response made me wonder if this was really happening. As the doctor prepared to insert a long needle into my abdomen, my husband questioned the need for an ultrasound since I was so close to delivery. Again, the doctor's response shocked us. Without looking up, he blurted, "Don't tell me how to do my job!" The needle went in and I watched as blood quickly filled the syringe.   Suddenly, a machine started beeping and a nurse cried, "His heart rate is dropping!" The doctor was supposed to pull amniotic fluid from the sac but instead poked our baby. Bursting through the door were two more nurses stepping into action. My arms were at my sides, one for blood pressure, the other being poked. Before I knew it, I was sucking in breaths from an oxygen mask as I watched through a haze the busy-ness that swirled about me.

After the baby and I were stabilized, we were left alone to rest. I had labored every day for the week prior to my entering the hospital. I would labor for another twelve hours before delivery. Because Luke was in a posterior position for so many hours he was born with a very bruised face. He spit up blood for the first three days of his life, which I attribute to the poke of the needle. Just after the delivery, this same doctor when stitching the episiotomy intentionally and unnecessarily placed one of those stitches in an inappropriate and sensitive area. It was a violating thing, which stole any possible joy from the experience of giving birth to a child. I was later to find out that I was not the only victim of his personal vendetta against women. We would be subpoenaed to testify against him ten years later.

## White Knuckles and Aching Hearts

Needless to say, I was deprived of what should have been a precious bonding time when our son, Luke, was born. I left the hospital aware of the new blessing of my child but feeling too heavy hearted to celebrate.

Luke would struggle constantly with respiratory issues that required a lot of special care. You could hear him from the other end of the house. His harsh breathing sounds would indicate our need to bundle him up in the middle of the night and go out into the cold. The harsh, cold Minnesota winters would serve to open his airways as we paced our little cul-de-sac under the stars.

My dad began to heal from his cancer experience and I from my terrible birth experience. We were both anxious to get back on our feet and do things for ourselves once again. It didn't take me long to realize that some of my energy would consistently have to go towards Luke's respiratory issues. He constantly got croup and we grew in the knowledge of how to take care of it. Jacob was always so healthy, so we were blazing new trails with this little one.

I walked through the double doors of the hospital breathing hard as I struggled to carry Luke. This one was over my head. I had tried all my tricks to treat his croup, and nothing had worked. He was fifteen months old and getting so heavy, but he was too sick to walk by himself. Heads turned to see where the seal-like sound was coming from. He made a different sound breathing in than he did breathing out, but both could be heard from across the room. Thankfully, I didn't even have to sit down because a doctor heard him, then saw him and came right over to me. Luke was instantly taken up to a room and the paper work was handled later.

After Luke had been in the hospital about four or five days, he took a turn for the worse. His little chest looked like it was breaking with every breath he was taking. He drifted in and out of sleep and his leg would suddenly spasm from his heart working so hard. He would have diarrhea suddenly and need to have his pajamas, sheets and everything cleaned up. People who would come to see him would get a noticeable look of fear on their faces and then try to conceal it.

We had one of our friends bring Jacob up to see his brother. Jake was only three and a half years old at the time. He walked in the door and lifted his head to see his brother in the tented crib. He whipped around, bolted out the door and down the hall. I raced out the door trying to find where he had gone. I asked a nurse if she had seen him. She pointed towards the patient playroom. I slowed down as I walked into the colorful, sterile room. There he was crouched in the corner behind a rack of toys. I went over and sat on the floor next to him. He buried his face in my chest and bawled. He didn't need to explain what he was feeling because I was feeling it too.

A couple of our dearest friends came up to the hospital and sang worship songs to our Lukey as he slept. The room was filled with the presence of the Lord. It was quite a moment. After they left, he endured his worst night yet. The nurses called for the doctor and he came to see us. He examined Luke and shook his head. He said that Luke's heart was being so overworked with every breath, he didn't think that he could make it like that for another twenty-four hours. He felt he needed to refer our case to another doctor who had further knowledge of respiratory issues.

When he left the room, it became dead silent.

## White Knuckles and Aching Hearts

Hanging onto the end of Luke's bed, I stared through the tent at my precious little one. I was choking back the tears at the thought of leaving the hospital without him. How would I survive such a thing? I was waiting for my husband to come to me and comfort me. When I looked up, I saw him reaching his hand in the little slit of the tent. He held onto Luke's foot and quietly cried a prayer to God. I saw tears dripping from his face. He needed as much comfort as I did. I went over to him and we swallowed each other in an embrace. We cried and begged Jesus to intervene. Kevin went to call family members with an update and I stayed behind. I looked at my little Lukey. I thought back to that terrible time of giving birth to him. His fifteen months of life had been filled with so many struggles.

I realized that as much as I loved him, I had never bonded with him when he was born. I had been so blessed by my first hours with Jacob after he was born. There is something so important about that bonding time. I crawled underneath the tent and into his crib. I pulled my baby close to my heart and I wailed in the only way I knew how. All of my pain and my fear broke loose as I struggled to hold Luke as close as possible.

He was unaware of the exchange I was having with him, as he was sleeping like a limp dishrag. I sat behind him and wrapped my arms around his tummy. I rested my head on his. His arms and legs just hung there and they didn't hug back. I stared at and studied every detail of this beautiful little lamb. I was in awe of the perfection of his fingers and his toes. His face had such a resemblance of us both and that made me smile.

What a gift God has given us in our children! We should never take them for granted or think for a moment that they will always be there. I stayed in his little crib until our hearts beat together with the same rhythm. I knew that he was a gift to me, but I also remembered that he was a gift from God. This gift was only temporarily mine. Luke ultimately belonged to his Father in heaven who cares for him far more than I ever could. I could not hang onto him with white knuckles and teach him anything of substance. This gift of my son was not to be on my terms, but on the terms of the One who created him. I knew this was true, but the process of letting that truth pass from my head to my heart seemed almost impossible. I knew that I had to open my hands and trust in my Jesus, no matter what.

I felt as though I had stepped off a cliff as I decided to trust the Lord with my fears. I released Luke and the outcome of his illness to the Lord and His peace swept over me.

*He calmed the storm to a whisper and stilled the waves* (Psalm 107:29).

CHAPTER FOUR

# Questions
# Without Answers

ithin twenty-four hours Luke experienced a complete turnaround. The new doctor prescribed the necessary medications and the countless prayers were heard in heaven. Before we realized what was happening, Lukey was tearing down the tent that covered his crib. I laughed at him and thanked God that his feisty personality was emerging once again.

As I reached up to "help" Luke take down his tent, I felt an unusual "pulling" in my stomach. I felt pretty sure that I was expecting our third child. When we were first married, we were going to wait about five years to have children. Thankfully, I became pregnant on our honeymoon, because it was during this pregnancy that I was found to have endometriosis. We needed to have our children right away.

I was right about my expecting and was experiencing a mixed bag of emotions. Because of the severe trauma to Luke's lungs, we were to keep him from running around too much at home. He was to gradually ease back into the life of a toddler. This was no small task, as Luke was not one to sit in one spot for very long. As I would watch he and Jake play with their toys, I rubbed my abdomen with thoughts of my baby growing inside of me. I realized how totally inadequate I was for the task at hand. At twenty-five years old, I felt like a child having a child. How scary it is to love someone so much, but realize you could lose him or her at any given moment. And yet to protect yourself from that kind of pain is to stop living altogether.

How do I do this Lord? How do I pour myself into the task of raising godly children and, at the same time, hold them with an open hand? If I cling too tightly, I will quench who they are. If I hold them too loosely, I will lose them for sure. There is obviously no going back, but what I have just seen, this past week, makes me wonder if I can survive what is out there in the great unknown.

## CHAPTER FIVE

# *Bumps, Bruises and Baggage*

ooking at me, you would never have known I was expecting or that I was worn out from the events of the previous couple years. I was about three months along in my pregnancy and, on the outside, looked pretty normal. Again I encountered a situation that was a catalyst for taking me deep into my wilderness journey. I was pushing my full grocery cart down the last aisle when I felt an unusual sensation that seemed all too familiar. I left my cart full of groceries at the store and drove home sobbing with fear and unbelief that this could possibly be happening again. Kevin tried hard to console me but I knew something was wrong. He took me in to the doctor and we found out that my cervix was softening and preparing for a miscarriage.

"This is the absolute earliest we can do this surgery, and of course, you know from experience, the potential risks involved." We sat there listening to the doctor with one part of our brain, while the other part tried figuring out what we would do about our boys, our bills and the rest of our lives. The doctor wanted to try the surgery again to see if we could hold the baby inside, had this happened even a week ago, he would not have been able to help us in this way. It would be possible to actually trigger a miscarriage, but without it, I would surely deliver way too early. The surgery went as planned and I was to stay in hospital for a week for observation.

Thankfully, I was able to leave the hospital after staying a week, and I was still pregnant. I needed to go home to strict bed rest for the next six months. I was to lay on my left side and only get up to go to the bathroom. This was difficult to do with two busy little boys to care for. We had many wonderful people from our church who chipped in to help us in our time of need. Imagine how old this must have gotten for them. They helped us through the three months of bed rest during my pregnancy with Luke, his delivery, his hospitalization and now six months of help caring for our boys and my husband. I felt so indebted to these people. I was overwhelmed by their kindness.

Money was becoming scarce along the way. Because of my endometriosis, I was unable to obtain good insurance. This onslaught of high-risk pregnancy problems brought with it a pile of medical debt. With every trip into the hospital to slow down contractions came another bill that would further set us back. I felt as though I had become a debt to society, not to mention our church family and immediate family. I watched Kevin work his tail off. He would go to work during the day, and many times have to leave to transport the boys from one place to the next. At night, he would care for our busy toddlers, clean the house and love me.

Our boys didn't know which way was up. One morning they would be at a loosely structured home, and that afternoon, they would be somewhere very strict. There were times when they just wanted to stay with me and I wanted them as badly. When they would leave crying, I would stay behind crying. I would pray and listen to great Christian music, but it brought little comfort. God seemed amazingly silent. The medicine I was on caused a restless, shaky feeling. I couldn't relax, nor could I get up and move around. I had to keep reminding myself that I was doing something very important. I was helping to spare the life of the priceless treasure growing inside of me. The nurses kept reminding me that if I delivered early, the baby could be blind or have cerebral palsy. I had no choice but to move forward by staying still.

How fair was this to my already growing toddlers? I couldn't bear that question. I needed to do what I was being called to do, and trust the Lord with their little hearts. Even though I couldn't feel Him, I knew Him to be faithful to His children.

After about three months of bed rest, I was feeling pretty depressed. It seemed like it would be forever before I could be the mother of my home and care for everyone the way I knew I could. Since I had gone a couple of days without contracting, my doctor said I could test the waters and get up. I was free! I got to see what the rest of the world was doing with their time. I headed to the quaint little town of Stillwater to meet my two dear friends from college.

Spending three months on your left side tends to make one weak and winded. I was six months along and desperately wanted some exercise. We decided to have lunch then take a walk along a path in the woods. We stopped periodically to take pictures and enjoy the beautiful fall colors. We all loved Jesus and used our time together to encourage and challenge each other in our faith. These two dear friends covered me with their prayers before we parted ways. It was such a wonderful day, but after only a couple of hours together I began to experience mild contractions. Well, it was fun while it lasted.

Back to bed I went for what would be the duration of the pregnancy. Within two weeks of my great adventure, some unusual things began to take place. When a friend who was visiting asked me where I had put my glass of water, I pointed and felt pins and needles shoot down my arm to my fingertips. I didn't say anything at that moment, but it scared me somewhat. Throughout the rest of the day I continued to feel numbing and tingling in that arm.

Over the next several days, more numbing came. The right side of my face went numb and I had a "crawling" feeling all over the back of my head. I knew something was very wrong but it seemed far too big for me to face. I decided my circulation was just getting bad because of the inactive lifestyle that I had to temporarily adhere to. Contractions would come and go, as did the neurological symptoms. Again I decided I was under such stress from keeping the baby in, that my nervous system was just "acting up." Yes, that's what it was—stress.

CHAPTER SIX

# *Spiritual Roots*

"Sure Mom, I promise! No boys, stay in and call you in the morning—I've got it!" I whipped out the door with my sleeping bag in one hand and my junk food in the other. This would be a fun slumber party with just a bunch of us eighth-grade girls. I felt especially excited to get there. We danced, ate and told stories for two hours. I was having a great time until a group of them decided to sneak out, meet some boys and make some memories. I knew I couldn't go along, so I didn't. There were only three of us who stayed behind. The other two I barely knew. They were joking back and forth about "end times" stories saying things like, "As if there will really be scorpions with poisonous stings and like people will want to die but won't be able to." I leaned in and listened hard.

I had never heard anything like this before. I knew God was very big and very near, but that was about it. I went outside and looked up at the stars and said something like this, "God, if there is more to you than I know, then teach me. I will read the Bible every day and you can somehow make it make sense to me. I don't want to miss out on anything. Thank you. Amen." In the days that followed, the Word of God came alive to me, and I grew into the knowledge of what it meant to be saved by the grace of God. I asked Jesus to take over my life and guide me all of my days. I became very passionate about my walk of faith—even as a teenager.

My quiet times have always been a priority. Not because I am so spiritual, but because I am so "not." I need Him so badly and without Him I quickly dry up and become self-absorbed. There were seasons in my life where I didn't abide as closely as I should. Of course, those were the times where I made my greatest mistakes. He never left me, though. His hand was always guiding me and protecting me.

I was so fortunate to have my college roommates Peggy and Patty (identical twins) love Jesus the way they did. We were all very "into" our quiet times and held each other accountable to our walk of faith.

Kevin and I married about a year after we met. As excited as I was, I was anxious about my quiet times becoming disrupted. This may sound odd, but it was a real concern for me. I had read much about the adjustment of two people becoming one.

Early one morning, the Lord spoke to my heart and told me that the quiet time is much like the tithe. Many wait until they have the money to give, but it never comes. But those who give what little they have, more will be given to them. In this same way, when one waits for the time to have their quiet time, it never comes. But to those who take the time for an encounter with the King, more time will be given.

That was just what I needed to hear! This is exactly what happened. My times alone with the Father proved to be the most precious part of my day. I added to my times of reading and praying by journaling. What a treasure this became! Anytime I began to wonder how we would get through something, I would just look back at one of my entries of struggle and triumph to remember that He would never forsake His own.

Each time I was about to give birth, I felt that same anxiety—but just for a moment. I remembered what He had told me years before. Even with little ones running around the house, I would still have time to read, write and pray. I was so used to God making Himself so real to me that I often wondered, *why doesn't everyone spend time with the Creator of the universe?* We rush around and try to do everything ourselves, not wanting to take a moment to talk with the One who has all the answers. This is so much like a toddler who doesn't want his mother's help to do the puzzle, when all she's waiting to do is to tell him that it's upside down.

These times with the Savior are where I learned how to pray—and listen—and wait. How awesome to have Jesus just a prayer away.

*Forever, O LORD, your word stands firm in heaven. Your faithfulness extends to every generation, as enduring as the earth you created. Your laws remain true today, for everything serves your plans* (Psalm 119:89-91).

## CHAPTER SEVEN

# *A Dark Dead End*

ou can imagine the disillusionment I began to feel when I would show up for my quiet time only to find stillness. No wind, no "sense," no voice. "Where are You, God?" I would pray.

Nothing.

"I am having such a hard time with this, can You please show me what You want from me?"

Quietness.

I began to fear that I had done something to chase my Lord away. When I asked Him what, I could hear no answer. Every once in a while when I would show up for my quiet time, some small verse would suddenly leap off the page at me! I would read on and the words seemed stale. Then I would go back to the original verse and it would somehow touch my soul. Food! I found food! I would underline, highlight and memorize the verse. I would look in the dictionary to find the expanded meaning of the key words in the verse. I would write my own paraphrase of what I thought the verse meant. It felt like I had suddenly eaten a piece of bread after a long fast. My mouth watered for more.

Each time I would show up for my quiet time, I expected something. Many times I would end up back on the verse that I found days ago. Other times, He would give me a new one. As I continued to experience disturbing amounts of numbing, pins and needles and sharp-shooting pains, I found myself more and more afraid. I was now entering month four in bed with this pregnancy. This meant that I was heading for two months of bed rest, the delivery of my baby, the recovery and then the endurance of some disease that would probably kill me.

Although my thinking was wrong, at this time in my life it was very much my reality. I felt so alone and it had seemed so long since I had heard from God. I had a friend visit me and she had just been with a woman in our church who suffered from multiple sclerosis. I lay there on my side as I listened to her tell me what life was like for this woman. She was once a very active athlete as I once was. She started out with mild numbing as I was now experiencing. My friend then said, "I guess it's personality types like yours that more often end up with multiple sclerosis." She dropped a bomb on me without even realizing it. When she left, the enemy of my soul tormented me with fear that was too dark for words. I was backing into my couch cushions as if he was backing me into a corner.

## A Dark Dead End

I couldn't get back any farther and I couldn't go any-where to get away. I just prayed out loud, "Help me, Jesus!" I cannot adequately describe the darkness and fear that came over me, but I knew that I was facing the enemy of my soul and my Lord seemed very far away. Lamenta-tions 3:7-9 gave words to what I was feeling.

*He has walled me in, and I cannot escape. He has bound me in heavy chains. And though I cry and shout, he shuts out my prayers. He has blocked my path with a high stone wall. He has twisted the road before me with many detours.*

I then picked up my journal and wrote: "Lord, why is my faith so small and my tolerance of hard things so short? ... A lot of people tell me that they could not handle what I am going through, and so I know it is a very hard thing that I am experiencing ... but I have a couple ques-tions. I feel like I have learned all that I can about not being in control and being helpless and dependent. Well, I guess I don't even know the meaning of it next to someone with a crippling disease ... but I wonder what it is that You are trying to teach me ... am I going to have to get a crippling disease to learn it??!!?? When I feel like I have taken all I can take, I fear that so much more awaits me—unless I learn what it is You want me to. That is so scary to me. I'd almost rather be shallow and live a more stable life than go through all of this. Lord, please minister to me."

*But those who wait upon the Lord will renew their strength; they shall run and not be weary, they will walk and not faint ... so don't you fear and don't you run, in this world of trials I have overcome* (words from a song by Dan Adler, based on Isaiah 40:31).

This was an important point in my faith walk. I suddenly knew that if I looked past my fears, I would see Jesus and somehow get through it. This wasn't great news to me though, because in my core I didn't want to suffer anymore. I did not have an eternal perspective. I had an earthly, momentary one. A small part of me saw that the way to peace (instead of fear) was to face the potential of a debilitating disease and know that Jesus would go with me there. The bigger part of me said, "No, Lord! No! Please, please please … I can't! I can't! I can't!" In all honesty, I vacillated back and forth from wanting to be in complete submission to the Lord's will for my life and wanting to avoid it at all costs.

## CHAPTER EIGHT

# Blessings and Boot Camp

y final months on bed rest came to a close when I went into labor three weeks early. It was a beautiful winter day and a perfect delivery. I only had to labor for three hours and our son, Jordan, came into the world to bless us all. I held him and looked out the window to whisper a prayer of thanks to my God. The snowflakes were falling and were as big and fluffy as cotton balls. I felt like the most blessed woman in the entire world. I had a devoted, loving husband and three beautiful sons. I was ready to begin really living.

*I will thank you, LORD, with all my heart; I will tell of all the marvelous things you have done. I will be filled with joy because of you. I will sing praises to your name, O Most High* (Psalm 9:1-2).

*The Lord is a shelter for the oppressed, a refuge in times of trouble. Those who know your name trust in you, for you, O LORD, have never abandoned anyone who searches for you* (Psalm 9:9-10).

"Keep that little one at home and visitors to a minimum. RSV is everywhere and your sons are at extra risk of contracting this virus. Everyone who visits is to be healthy and is to wash their hands before holding the baby." We listened intently to our doctor's instructions. Every mother knows what those first days at home are like with a little one. Nights are days to the newborn, and yet the days are a party waiting to happen for the toddlers who have gotten a full night's sleep. Those days became sort of a blur and the goal was to simply get through them and get on a schedule. I did my best keeping things clean, keeping everyone fed and keeping everyone healthy. As exhausted as I was, I just loved being up and around again.

As I would get up at night every other hour to feed my little one, I would continually deny the fact that I was experiencing more and more symptoms. There were times when I felt as if a spear was going through my leg or my foot. My elbows and knees hurt for some time. The facial numbing and "crawling" feeling continued. Maybe I could "outrun" it. I had a big job to do and maybe, if God saw how hard I worked at being a good mom, He would take away these irritating symptoms—and the underlying fear.

My best efforts to keep things clean and healthy failed. The virus found its way into our home and within a couple days, Luke was extremely ill. The ER doctor said that because this was an airborne virus and we had a new-born baby, we would be better off treating Luke at home. He didn't want us taking our baby in and out of the cold to a hospital full of sick children. We put a playpen down stairs and covered it with a blanket to make a "tent" for him. We then were blowing the steamer in through the side of the playpen. I learned how to do the bronchial draining by pounding on the sides of his chest. For the next few weeks, my life would consist of sleep deprivation, disinfectant, a long hallway and two hooks to hang the shirts I wore for each child. I did Luke's drainage, disinfected my hands, changed my shirt and nursed the baby. Again, I would disinfect my hands, change my shirt and take care of Luke. Back and forth, back and forth—all day, all night, every two hours. I felt like a zombie who was going through the motions. I would drag myself down the hall with heavy legs and burning eyes. One night both boys slept for three hours and I actually got up and cleaned the house. My body had the illusion of rest because the extra hour was more than I was used to. My hands became cracked and dry from all the hand washing. I really didn't know how long I could last at this pace. Again, the symptoms were there and escalating, but they were the least of my concerns at this time.

I grabbed the bottle of formula and whipped down the hallway to get Jordan from his crib. I poked my head into his room to see him coughing so hard his back was arching up like a cat. There was no sound coming from his mouth and his lips turned as blue as his little sleeper with every cough. He was so tiny and fragile, and it concerned me to hear that familiar "whistle" when he would breathe.

We were involved in a small group through our church. I called them and asked them to come over and pray for us. I didn't know how much more I could handle. As our friends filed in and found their spots, I sat on the floor of our living room with my elbows on my knees—my bare knees. I needed a new pair of jeans. One of our friends played the song by Steven Curtis Chapman, "His Strength is Perfect." It hit home in such a powerful way as it reminded me that even when my strength is gone, His is perfect and able to carry me through.

The group then gathered around baby Jordan and laid hands on him. He was literally covered up by all the praying hands. God's power invaded that room and we felt sure that we were on the cusp of experiencing a true miracle.

We walked through the same double doors and were dealing with the same illness as we were ten months ago, but this time I was carrying my four-week-old into the hospital. The doctor whisked in and asked us what the problem was. We talked to the side of his face while he examined our baby. He then looked up and spouted, "Well, his ears look fine and his lungs sound fine." He was giving us the impression that he was waiting for us to make room for the next patient.

I looked at him and said, "I would like a second opinion please."

He was taken back a bit and asked "What?" I repeated what I had said. Out he went and then we waited some time for the next doctor to come in.

This doctor examined Jordan more closely and with greater care. He looked up at us and said, "Your son has double ear infections and double pneumonia. We're going to need to admit him." I told him that I knew that and let him know of the previous doctor's diagnosis. He said something to the effect that he has learned never to discount a mother's opinion about her child.

## Blessings and Boot Camp

As I followed the nurse to Jordan's room, my eyes caught a glimpse of the room where Luke stayed about ten months ago. It was two doors down. At first, things were very busy with nurses hooking up all of the gadgets, dosing the medicines and putting on Jordan's baby hospital pajamas. Then all of a sudden we were alone and it was quiet. I pulled up a rocking chair and plopped down when something very unexpected happened. An unexplainable peace came over me. Even though we were in the midst of a cold, Minnesota winter, I felt as if I had thrown my head back and absorbed the warmth of the sun on that first warm day of spring.

What was this about? I wasn't sure, but I knew that I was being flooded with peace and I was right where I was supposed to be. This must be what the Bible means when it tells of "peace that passes understanding" because I sure didn't understand why I felt the way I did. After one week at the hospital, we took our baby home. He had actually lost weight in the hospital because he wasn't nursing.

Even though we had endured four weeks of those "new born nights," we were starting from scratch as far as the nightly feedings went. Did you know that brainwashing is accomplished by sleep deprivation? All of your ability to reason or think clearly goes out the window when there is no sleep. Our bodies are designed to take in, put out and rest. When there is no rest, there is no balance and systems break down.

If it were possible for your heart to just stop beating from exhaustion, I thought mine would. I am sure that my immunities were taking a beating at least. This would be another detour that sent me deeper into the wilderness of my life.

CHAPTER NINE

# *Dark Days, Lost Ways and Precious Love*

think, I mean … where was, ah, … I mean I saw her … um today might, I should …" I mumbled aimlessly.

"Susie, hang up the phone right now, I am calling Kevin!" My brain was in a fog and my confusion scared my sister. I hung up the phone and feared the worst was yet to come. I sat there on my couch and stared straight ahead. My whole face pulsated with numbness. My eye twitched constantly. I was beyond myself with exhaustion and my whole body ached. Meanwhile, my three little ones played in the next room unaware of what was happening with me. I'm not sure, but I think they were dumping the corn flakes on the ground and dancing in them again.

Kevin raced in the door and up the stairs. He asked me what was wrong. I couldn't speak, I could only cry quietly. Then I said, "I am sorry, honey. I am so sorry, something is really wrong with me. I am sorry."

He just said, "It'll be okay," and held me close. He swooped me up in his arms and brought me to the hospital. They ran all the tests they could and covered me up because I was shivering. When the doctor pulled Kevin aside, I could still hear him. He told Kevin that they had done as much as they could do there, and he needed to take me home and start scheduling some appointments. A couple of the things he was concerned about were a brain tumor or multiple sclerosis.

I was completely defeated. I had lost. I could not outrun the enemy of my soul and the sky felt dark once again.

The drive home was the darkest hour of my life. So the possibilities for my life were death or watching others live a full life while I watched from the sidelines. I wanted neither.

More quiet, less tears—just emptiness.

Was the Lord disappointed in me? Someone told me that I probably had some hidden sin in my life and if I would just confess it, maybe this would all go away. I searched my heart and was at a complete loss. I allowed myself to wonder if He was disappointed or just too busy to help me. I could almost bear the thought of disappointment more than the thought of Him being too busy or uninterested. Where was He? I had so many plans for my life. I had so many great ideas for parenting these three precious boys. Wasn't that noble enough? "Even if I bug You, God, can't You see how much these boys need their mother? Please speak to me."

Kevin pulled into our driveway and carried me into the house. I let him carry me as I rested my head on his shoulder. He is so big and strong, and yet so tender, patient and devoted. He did not deserve this. When he tucked me in bed I grabbed his arms and said, "You have my permission to divorce me. I will go live with my parents." My voice cracked and I lost it once again. Through my relentless tears I ordered him, "You be sure to marry someone who is active and will play with the boys. She has to love Jesus, have a sense of humor and be available for them. I don't think I can let them see me like this. You have given more than your share to me and I can't ask you to give me any more." He interrupted my tearful plea by kneeling down at my bedside and brushing the hair out of my eyes. He stared at me and waited for me to quiet down.

As I lay there in bed with him kneeling at my side, we held each other's shoulders like we were caught in a raging river not wanting to lose each other. He then said something that I will never forget. He said, "You are my bride and you always will be, and if I have to kneel down to kiss you because you're in a wheelchair, then that's what I will do"

For the first time in a long time, I was speechless. I was blown away by his love for me and it taught me much of what Jesus' love, the costly kind, was all about. What can I say? As I write this, I am still driven to tears by his amazing love. I was begging God to intervene and show me something of Himself. He chose to reveal His love for me through my husband. Kevin was not speaking from the emotion of the moment. He had already been carrying around with him the heaviness of the events from the past year. He knew how costly and how enduring his commitment would be.

*Love is patient and kind .... Love does not demand its own way. Love is not irritable, it keeps no record of when it has been wronged .... Love never gives up, never loses faith, is always hopeful, and endures through every circumstance. Love will last forever* (1 Corinthians 13:4-8).

## CHAPTER TEN

# *Battles Large and Small*

Our families were waiting anxiously to hear what was wrong with me. Kevin went to the kitchen to call everyone. As I lay there in bed and listened to him talk to our family members, I became frozen with fear of what lay ahead for me. We scheduled our appointments and tried to "do" life as best as we could. By this stage of the game, many of our friends had to get back to living their own lives. I wanted to be the one to care for my family, but it became extremely difficult. Between sleepless nights with the baby, busy days with toddlers and an increasing list of symptoms, I weakly walked through the days.

My boys were active and happy. They blazed through each day not wanting to miss a thing. My symptoms would come and go. I felt happiest on the days when the scary symptoms went somewhere else and I was only left with terrible fatigue. On these days, I would soak up the "normal" days of being a mother with little ones. When the symptoms would return bringing another one along, I felt cornered and afraid. There were times when I felt as if the enemy of my soul had my face clenched in his hand while he spewed out the question, "Where is your God now, huh? I have got you by the face and there is no one to help you!"

I felt like a soldier whose plane had gone down in enemy territory. I was feeling as though I was without armor, without protection and without anyone to fight for me. Many times during these moments, the phone would ring with a bill collector on the other end of the line. We were going broke and we still didn't know what was wrong with me! Kevin and I both came into our marriage with great credit. It was so hard to see this area of our life completely turned upside down. There is so much shame surrounding money problems.

The day arrived when I was to see the neurologist. I had a certain peace inside, but it was so buried under self-induced fear and stress that I didn't get to enjoy it much. The doctor was a bit irritated that we had our three, active boys along. Getting a sitter for this appointment wasn't even close to being a possibility. After he examined me, he was certain that this was not multiple sclerosis. He said that on the surface it could look like that because of the numbing, dizziness, pain and fatigue. But with MS the numbing doesn't come and go in the way that I was experiencing.

Hallelujah! I could have jumped across the room and swallowed this doctor in a bear hug, but I got the feeling he was ready for us to leave. "Thank You, thank You Jesus!"

## Battles Large and Small

During our ride home Kevin wondered why I was so happy. He reminded me that we still needed to find out what was wrong. I told him that having MS would have meant that I would have to live life on the sidelines. If I had a brain tumor, I would either get it operated on, or die, but I wouldn't be forced to live at half strength like I had been doing. I really thought this was okay thinking until he got upset with me. He asked, "What are you talking about? You can't accept death over life that easily. We need you here." I was surprised by his response and knew then that my thinking was pretty selfish. (I have since learned much about brain tumors and know that many live brutal lives as a result of them.) We still did not know what was wrong with me, but it seemed that the more I was able to sleep at night, the better I would feel. I actually began to exercise again and, even though it took a lot out of me, it felt good. I had started teaching aerobics after our first son was born. It had been ages since I thought of anything but high-risk pregnancies, babies, hospitals and sickness.

## Chapter Eleven

# *Roller Coaster Rides and Miracles*

y health continued to be a roller coaster ride. Up and down and all around. During my "up" times, I was beside myself with joy, thinking the sickness was all in my head and it really was going away. When the symptoms came flooding back in, the dark cloud came with them. Here was one of my journal entries during a more hopeful time:

5/9/90: "Lord, I feel like I am still in the healing process over what has happened in the last several months. I want so much to be whole, restored and strong again. I feel "almost" there … but these numbing spells still scare me so. Please deliver me from whatever is causing it and from that constant fear of terminal illness. I know it's not from You. I thank You for my beautiful family. I cherish them so very much. Kevin is the sweetest, most tender, loving husband

and father there is. Jacob is so neat and sweet—he's so full of love, he is a great big brother. Lukey has such a colorful personality, he is so tender and yet so strong willed ... and Jordan is so very sweet. It seems like he has a little of both boys in him. I love them all so much. How blessed I am! I love you, Lord, and I plead my case before you for complete and total healing. Amen."

And from one of those darker moments: "Please, Lord, rescue me from this trial ... I have had enough. The past two years have been so very hard ... I need to rest. Please set me upon higher ground and make my footsteps firm. Please give me some peace and faith. I need to hear from You. I am totally at a loss."

During one of the more dark times I just couldn't stand it anymore. No one knew what was wrong with me. This caused some to invalidate the fact that I was sick. I even invalidated myself at times. I needed to know where this thing would take me. If I was going to live, I wanted to fight with everything in me. If I was dying, I wanted to let go of things that I was exhausting myself over. I bowed and prayed, "Lord, You know what is wrong with me. I need You to tell me if I am living or dying. Please have someone call me today and point me in the right direction. I love You. Amen."

*Rrrrring.* The phone instantly rang upon the completion of my prayer. "Susie, are you still having all of that numbing and stuff?" It was a man from our small group. When I replied that I was, he said, "Turn on channel four. I have to go. See ya!" I turned on the television to see an amazing sight. There sat a panel of women who thought for the longest time that they had either a brain tumor or MS! They described their symptoms as if they had been my own! I couldn't believe my ears. These women all had one thing in common—they suffered from Lyme disease. I held my stomach for the longest time and just rocked back and forth between sobs.

I was feeling validated, amazed at God's communication with me, and afraid of the sight of some of these crippled women. I went to the doctor and asked to be tested for Lyme disease. The nurse said, "You know, your symptoms do point in that direction. I will see if we can get you started right away on a low dose of antibiotics." We discussed the approximate time that my symptoms surfaced and we traced it back to that one day in Stillwater with my friends. It was shortly after that when the first numbing spells came. She then said, "Well, if you were bit during your pregnancy, we will have to get your baby tested. How is his health? Does he seem to be feeling okay?" She was interested to hear that he was very sick at four weeks of age, but since then had been a high-energy, moving-all-the-time sort of kid. She asked more about his hospital stay and what kind of treatment he received. I told her that he was on intravenous medicine for the whole week he was in the hospital.

It appears that the time we admitted Jordan into the hospital, when I was feeling that warmth in my soul, was the very thing that was saving his life. I have since heard stories of babies who have died from being in the womb when the mother was infected with Lyme. Isn't it amazing how we shake our fists at God as if we know better than He does? How does He endure our sin? We want what we want, when we want it. We all wanted Jordan to get better that night in our living room when our small group prayed. We really felt the Lord's presence and expected Him to do great things.

He did a far greater thing than we were asking of Him. He saved my Jordan's life. He endured our questions of "Why?" "How long?" and "What for?" knowing full well that we would see in time. Recorded below is one of those break-through moments in my wilderness journey. The Lord was teaching me how to survive in the midst of the darkness—and the lions and tigers and bears.

6/90: "I was tucking Jacob in bed and saying his prayers last night. After kissing Luke and him on the forehead, I headed out the door. Jacob said, 'Mom, do you wanna know how much I love God?'

"I replied, 'I'd love to know. '

"He stretched his arms out as far as they could go and said, 'This much.'

"I told him how wonderful that was and added, 'Do you want to know how much He loves you?'

"'Yes,' he said.

"I proceeded to say, 'Higher than the sky, farther than the farthest ocean … He loves us more than that.'

"He rocked back on his knees and said, 'Wow!' I told them both I loved them and tucked them in. Just when I got to the doorway I turned around to see Jacob doing actions to a song he'd learned in preschool. Waving his arms around to emphasize the words he shouted, 'There's nothing my God cannot do … for you!!!' He was singing to me and pointing to me when his song ended.

"I stood there with my four-year-old pointing at me and I noticed that familiar lump in my throat. I blinked back my tears and said, 'I think I am finally learning that. Good night, honey.' Praise the Lord!"

*Shout with joy to the LORD, O earth! Worship the LORD with gladness. Come before him, singing with joy. Acknowledge that the LORD is God! He made us, and we are his. We are his people, the sheep of his pasture. Enter his gates with thanksgiving; go into his courts with praise. Give thanks to him and bless his name. For the LORD is good. His unfailing love continues forever, and his faithfulness continues to each generation* (Psalm 100).

## CHAPTER TWELVE

# Becoming a Warrior... Part-Time

The numbing remained and yet it became clear to me that "sicknesses flee at His voice" and that God was in complete control. "When He decides it is time, it will be removed from me, whether in this life or in heaven. Praise His name."

Again from my journal: "… each time when the numbing comes and causes fear … I am to stand against it in the name of Jesus. I will resist the devil and his spirit of fear. I acknowledge that Jesus is my King and the devil has to flee."

On top of this, the Lord allowed me to open up to this amazing Scripture: *"For the power of the wicked will be broken, but the LORD upholds the righteous"* (Psalm 37:17, NIV).

I felt that I had received a valuable weapon for warfare in the wilderness. We can't always control the battles that come our way, but we can do something about the effect they have on our soul. The enemy will pull out every stop to make us believe a lie when we are down. It is up to us to decide if we will invite these lies in to sup, or to stop them from ever taking up residence in our core belief system. For me, faith happened when I spent less time worrying about my circumstance and more time praying about the condition of my heart.

> *Pay attention, my child, to what I say. Listen carefully. Don't lose sight of my words. Let them penetrate deep within your heart, for they bring life and radiant health to anyone who discovers their meaning. Above all else, guard your heart, for it affects everything you do* (awesome!) (Proverbs 4:20-23).

Because I was prone to fear, doubt and worry, I didn't always remember this blessed truth. The doctor tested me for Lyme disease and put me on a three-month dose of antibiotics. The test came back negative and I was temporarily taken back a bit. But then my husband reminded me that these tests were inconclusive. He further reminded how clearly I had heard God on that day of the phone call.

The antibiotics basically broke my fall. I just stopped getting worse and worse. This was a relief to me and I did my best to function at about 50 percent strength. When my medicine was almost gone, I began to get a little nervous. I could tell that the disease still had the upper hand on me. Within a few weeks of being off of the medicine, I relapsed worse than I had been yet. I wrote:

9/14/90: "Lord it has been a long time since I have written again. You have given me a sense that I am going to be totally healed ... and yet it seems that my numbing is getting worse again. It has been about three years of back to back crises and I am weary. I need a fresh touch from You. I'm not sure I know what faith and trust is about anymore. I long to be restored. Please do something. Amen."

9/19/90: "Lord, as You know, the numbing has lightened up somewhat and I feel like I've been given Your peace. Thank You so much. I wait for full restoration from You, O Lord. But I thank You for Your peace in the midst of it all. My soul waits on the Lord. I love You and exalt You as my king, my physician and healer. You are in complete control and I will follow You forever. You are my strength—restore me to a level path. Amen."

## CHAPTER THIRTEEN

# *Battles Without Armor*

I loved the infectious disease doctor I was referred to. His name was Dr. Kind and he really was. He had successfully treated other Lyme patients and I was glad to be there. My test came back positive this time, which was quite validating. The combined medicines he prescribed made me feel like I could actually "do life." I had not felt this good since before my pregnancy. I had mild symptoms and pain, but mostly I was functional. I was even able to teach an occasional aerobics class! This helped me mentally and even contributed a little to our desperate financial situation. This blessed time lasted about three months.

Sweating bullets…I anxiously watched my medicine slowly run out. I knew that I still had not won the battle against this disease. I was just in a holding pattern. The doctors had to stick to this three-month treatment for the sake of my kidneys. The kidneys needed a break and a chance to recover from being overloaded.

A friend stopped by to see how we were holding up. As she told me how her job was going my face began to pulsate with numbness. "So anyway, they changed my hours… " my friend continued. (*Please no more symptoms—please God.*) "…and I just love my co-workers, they are all so fun." (*Can she tell that my eye is twitching again? Please symptoms, go away!*) "…and I want to get this cute outfit from Daytons…" (*Dizziness, heavy legs… it's all coming back. Please, God, have mercy!*) I tried to listen but felt severely distracted.

Within two weeks of going off of the medicine, I experienced the worst relapse yet. My symptoms snowballed and I felt as though I was falling into a deep, dark pit. At night when everyone would be sleeping, I would feel prickly sensations in my hands and feet. I would feel as if that spear was going through my thigh again. The crawling and numbing sensation would start in the back of my head and work it's way to my face. Nighttime was my own private time of torment. I didn't want to wake Kevin because he was so overworked and needed his rest. Although sometimes, I just had to have him pray for me or I would have been swallowed up by fear.

I would strategically use my energy on the things I absolutely needed to. One day I had propped myself against the counter as I prepared cereal and juice for my three active, little boys. My body felt heavy even though my weight had gone down to 99 pounds. My brain was foggy and the ever present facial numbing gave me the sensation that I had a big growth on my face. One at a time, I carried the bowls of cereal and glasses of juice to the table. I had one boy in a high chair, one in a booster chair and one sitting on a phone book. As I stood there answering questions and pushing juice glasses away from the edge of the table, I found myself feeling terribly weak. I looked over into the living room and decided it was too far away to travel, especially if the boys needed me back here any time soon.

I decided to lay down on the floor right where I was and just rest a bit. It felt so good to get off my feet. I took in a big breath and released it as I rested. I noticed all of the crayon marks under the table. Just then things got a little hectic on top. Jake and Luke were singing a song with wild actions and they knocked a bowl of cereal down on top of me. At first they giggled at the sight of their mom covered in corn flakes and milk. But as I lay there covered in a mess that was so beyond what I had energy for—I sobbed. The two older boys crawled down from their chairs and put their arms around me. This moment had sort of summed up what I felt my life had become.

Some mornings, I would beg Kevin to stay home from work. I would hold onto his hands and ask him to stay just for a while. As he would gently, yet firmly, peel my fingers off his arm, he would tell me he really needed to work so we could pay our bills. I would then ask, "What if this is the day? What if this is the day that I just drop and die and the kids are left all alone?" This was not a manipulative question. I sincerely wondered every day if that would be the day when I would just fall over and die. My health felt so unstable and fragile. Once my mornings were the best part of my day... they had now become a mockery to me because they represented declined health.

*It is a land as dark as midnight, a land of utter gloom where confusion reigns and the light is as dark as midnight* (Job 10:22).

# CHAPTER FOURTEEN

# *Angels With Skin On*

I had two angels in my life who added to the love and support my husband was giving me. I served with Peggy on the women's ministry committee at our church. She was about thirty-five years older than me and was truly a mentor She took me under her wing and taught me much about the Savior. Peggy was fighting cancer at the same time that I was battling Lyme disease.

We would call each other and pray over the phone whenever one of us was down. Usually we felt bad at opposite times, which allowed us to help the other through the valley experiences. Peggy had a strong sense that she was not going to make it, and that I was to be healed.

That was so hard for me to hear. She often said, "The Lord will take me when He gets more glory from my death than He does from my life." She would take her gentle, weathered hand and touch the side of my face that was numb and ask Jesus to intervene on my behalf. She was an amazing example of living for Jesus and being accountable to His principles whether in fullness or emptiness, in sickness or in health, in abundance or in poverty. She was marked by love and always had her Savior on her mind.

At her funeral, even her husband was overwhelmed by the masses who came to honor her memory. Person after person got up to speak of the gifts of love and generosity they had received from Peggy. He never knew just how many hungry people she fed and prayed for. He was blown over by the humility in which she gave herself away. Her whole life pointed to Jesus. I can't wait to see her again.

Thank You, Lord Jesus, for the blessing of Peggy. I learned so much from her and she was such a good friend. I am so glad she is enjoying Your presence. Help me to be a woman of integrity like she was, Lord. I am better for knowing her. Amen.

I often describe Betsy as an angel with a crooked halo. She is such a treasure to me! We served together on the Mercy Team, a ministry birthed from our women's ministry committee. It was set up for people in crisis. We had teams of people to come around a family in various ways—assisting with meals, child care, prayer and visitation. The crises were so varied that we were often learning as we went along.

Our friendship solidified during this time and is still a great source of strength for both of us. She has two wonderful dimensions to her personality. On one hand, she can hear the Spirit of God unlike anyone I have ever known. It has been an honor to minister with her and learn about listening to God. The Lord has used her in countless ways to bring truth to desperate situations. It has been amazing to watch Him do His work through her. The other side of her is a feisty, somewhat rebellious person whom the Lord needs to constantly remind that she's not in charge. When she would intercede on my behalf about the spirit of fear that I struggled with, she would get so mad at the enemy of my soul.

It seemed that if you could have seen him in the flesh while she was praying, you would have seen her lunge at him and take him to the floor. Her heart is so precious and she loves Jesus so much. There have been many more desperate situations that we have carried each other through and I will always love her.

Thank You, thank You, Jesus, for the gift of Betsy. She is such a blessing to the body of Christ and even more so to me. Keep on speaking to her in such great detail, and keep on reminding her who's in charge (hee hee). I will always be grateful for her forever friendship. Amen.

I remember one time when Betsy and a couple other friends came to our home to help Kevin with the housework. It never grew easier for me to have people working around me cleaning, while I lay in bed. Betsy somehow made it tolerable. She was never one to falsely flatter or to "gush" all over someone.

Betsy vacuumed and dusted my room. I was wearing my usual boxers and T-shirt and lying on top of the covers because I was warm. She glanced over at me and said, "Man, you have such cute, muscular legs." I should have just accepted the compliment and left well enough alone.

I added, "But my feet are so ugly. My dad used to tease me about these feet."

She replied, "They can't be any worse than anyone else's. Let me see 'em." When I put my leg in the air for her to see my foot she smirked. "Yeah, I guess they are uglier than average ... they sort of look like a bird's claws!" I started to laugh and couldn't stop. This made her laugh as she sat down beside me. Because I am the type to "gush," I did. I told her how very dear she was to me and thanked her for never giving up on me. We had prayed each other through so much and yet this battle seemed so lopsided. She carried me many more miles than I had ever carried her. I did not know how I would have survived without her persistent faith to borrow from. She battled for me and with me and is my forever friend.

As Betsy sat at my bedside and our laughter quieted, it became apparent that she had something serious to say to me. She held my hand with both of hers and said, "You know that it's not over yet, don't you? Do you know that you will get worse before you get better?" I stared up at her with tears escaping out the sides of my eyes. I nodded in agreement sensing and now knowing that a bigger battle was awaiting me. She said, "The Lord has told me this, that your sickness will take a turn for the worse, but you are not to be afraid. Trust Him in the darkness and He will surely save you. Hang onto Him with everything you have and you will see Him work. You will be delivered from this, but not without a fight." She prayed right then and there for me to have the courage to face the days ahead. I had a peace inside because I knew I wasn't going into this blindly. I would come out the other side and be restored, whatever that would mean.

*But you, O Lord, are a merciful and gracious God, slow to get angry, full of unfailing love and truth. Look down and have mercy on me. Give strength to your servant; yes, save me, for I am your servant* (Psalm 86:15-16).

## Chapter Fifteen

# *Messengers from Heaven*

ven though I wrestled so much with the unknown, my Lord comforted me. He sent me messengers who would ground me and help me stay focused on the things of God. One such messenger came in the form of a phone call. A long-lost friend called and said, "I know we have lost touch but I have heard of your plight and have been praying for you. I believe the Lord is using your pain to build a platform from which you will speak someday. Lean into the pain and learn all you can from it."

Wow, could it be? Could this actually be building something in me that would help others? God's Word promises me that my tears and trials will not be in vain. This became a wonderful glimmer of hope.

Around that time a lady approached me in church. I

was a bit leery because of some of the comments I had received up to this point. She said, "You don't know me, but I have heard of your struggle. I took it back to my mom's Bible study and the ladies have been praying for you. We believe that the Lord is going to heal you. Because we are human and may have heard wrong, we are praying for three unrelated confirmations to come to you this week."

I was so tired and pretty afraid to get my hopes up so I said, "Thank you for praying; I really appreciate it."

The next day I was meditating on the Scripture, "... and your recovery will spring speedily forth ..." (Isaiah 58:8), when the phone rang. It was my sweet Betsy. She was praying for me and opened up to a Scripture, which happened to be the same one I was reading at the time. She then said, "I really believe that the Lord is going to heal you in the land of the living."

Coming from her, this meant so much because she was never one to tell me what I wanted to hear if it wasn't from God. I wasn't even thinking about this being "Confirmation #1." I just was excited to hear her say that she was sensing this. A couple days later, I received a call from someone that I did not know very well. She said she felt real hesitant to call me and tell me this. "You can't be mad at me if I am wrong about this, I mean, I didn't want to call you in the first place. I just knew I'd be miserable if I didn't tell you ... well ... "

I finally asked, "... tell me what?"

She then said, "Okay, well, I feel like I am supposed to tell you that your going to be healed ... but if your not, you can't get mad at me because I didn't want to call you in the first place!" It was humorous. I thanked her for having the guts to call and told her what had happened to me in church the previous Sunday. I hung up the phone, sat back in my chair and whispered, "Thank You, thank You, Lord."

The most recent relapse had completely knocked me off my feet. My days were filled with parenting three little ones from the couch. I could only get up when I absolutely had to. I had a dizzy spell that lasted a couple months. I would lie there and the room would feel like it was spinning. I felt off balance and the right side of my face felt heavier than the left side. All I could do was endure until Kevin came home from work. Then I would go to bed and pray myself to sleep.

I remember one specific time when some friends brought a meal over to help us out. I was half asleep and yet I could hear their voices. It had occurred to me how much energy they must have to fluctuate their voices that way. The littlest things seemed to take up so much energy. Even though I had received those precious words of healing, it seemed it would be real easy to just let go and stop breathing. Death didn't feel that far out of reach. Every time I would offer up the prayer for instant healing, it would seem to bounce off the ceiling and land back on top of me.

It finally became unbearable and my doctor requested that I come to the hospital to get started on IV therapy. Kevin carried me out to the car and we stopped to pick up my mom. A friend at work told her it was pretty painful to have the shunt put in for this kind of treatment. Her friend's daughter had passed out when they put this tube-like needle into her vein. Needless to say, she was quite worried about the whole thing. I was so glad to have her with me—she has always loved me so much.

We arrived at the hospital and walked through the double doors labeled Cancer Treatment Center. They put me in a hospital gown and asked me to lie down. I asked to use the restroom first. I went in there, put my face in my lap and just wailed. I was so sick and tired of being sick and tired. I didn't know how much more I could take. There seemed to be no end to my sobs and my mom could hear me through the door. She came into the bathroom, stood me up and put my head on her shoulder. She held me there and told me to just let it all out. I couldn't contain myself. She gradually walked me over to the hospital bed and tucked me in.

I instantly felt like I was dozing off. The nurse was trying to keep my attention so she could explain what she was about to do. She needed to teach me how to hook up and unhook my IV bags. I was trying to listen but I had used up all of my energy crying in the bathroom. The nurse decided to teach Kevin so that he could teach me later. As the nurse inserted the shunt in my arm, my mom took a breath. I didn't even budge. I was so exhausted it didn't seem worth my energy to move. For the next month, I would have to go in every couple of days to receive a new shunt due to veins that would collapse. Each time was a painful experience.

They sent us home with our equipment and said that the IV bags would be delivered to our house. The whole top level of our refrigerator was packed with bags of medicine. We used a hanger and hooked the meds on our mini blinds. The doctor warned us that this medicine was so strong that some were unable to stay on it because it made them too sick. I was determined not to be one of those people. He also said that it would wage war on this disease by circulating through my body and bringing up all the "pockets" of bacteria and then take them on. I was going to feel my symptoms in their fullest form.

Two days after I received "Confirmation #2," my oldest son came home from kindergarten. He hopped up on my bed to talk to me while I was receiving an IV treatment. This seemed so backwards to me because I was suppose to be the one greeting him at the door, going through his backpack and reading him stories. This was too hard for me, so it was the other way around for us. Once when I complained to Betsy about this, she said to me, "Don't you know that God is sovereign and He knows just what He is doing? Did you ever think that in a world where men and boys do not know how to treat women and girls, that maybe the Lord is raising your boys up and teaching them His way by seeing how their dad serves you? Let the Lord do His thing in all of your lives!"

Needless to say, I stood confronted and knew that she was right. So this particular day when Jacob hopped up next to me and pulled out his wrinkled papers, I really tried to see God's will in it all. It didn't take long because I was about to hear the voice of God through a little child—my child.

Jacob said, "Mommy, I did not listen very well in school today."

"Why not?" I asked.

"Because I was listening to God instead." He had my full attention. He then added, "He told me that He was going to heal you and make you all better. I even drew a picture of it. See here, this is you standing on the grass on a bright sunny day … and see how happy you are? That's 'cause Jesus made you all better."

This picture was straight from heaven. It was almost prophetic that he had me standing on green grass. Many times I had described our years of struggle as a winter-like wilderness journey. I was so blessed by this gift from my

Jacob. I pulled him close and thanked him for listening to God for me.

He replied, "Sure … ah, what's there to eat?" Out of the mouths of babes.

"Confirmation #3" came to me through my precious little boy. Could we possibly serve a more loving and personal God? I had a sense that my healing was a ways off, but I knew this—it would surely come.

CHAPTER SIXTEEN

# *Statements of Faith*

ournal entry 10/20/90: "My soul waits for the Lord more than the watchman waits for the morning. Lord, I love You ... I do ask for healing in Your timing, and for the grace to make it through. You are a mighty and awesome God, You are a mighty warrior and I love You so much. Anoint my head with oil and make my cup run over. Protect us from the evil one. Amen."

11/16/90: "Holy God, You are so very mighty and wonderful. You are totally in control. We have such a limited capacity to grasp that. Your mighty hand upholds me and I love You so very much. The fire surrounds us and yet we remain unburned. Financially, we are really hurting, and the Lyme continues to be a battle ... and yet my God in the midst of Thee is mighty. I love You. Amen."

11/21/90: "Lord, these are the days I need You to remind me that You are taking care of us. I am lacking sleep, battling

Lyme disease and financially, we are just dying. I can't believe this. This has all been going on for so long. I know You're there. Please hold my hand and give me Your peace. We do have so much to be thankful for. I love You. Amen."

You would have thought that this part of the sickness would have been the most difficult, but it wasn't. It was much harder to be mostly sick and still have three busy little ones to care for. All of the spills and colds and fights seemed so beyond what I had energy for. When I finally got to the point where I could do nothing but rest in bed, I actually experienced more moments of peace and prayer. Up to this point, I had tried everything I could, to get God to do what I wanted Him to. I had cried, begged, pleaded, negotiated, screamed and swore, but He would not rescue me from this long journey. Looking back, I am so thankful that God allowed me the process of learning something of His ways. His silences in the midst of my begging for answers put to rest any notion that there is a formula or program by which He is bound.

One day as I lay on the couch hooked up to my I.V., which was hooked up to the mini blinds, I looked around and sighed. Our dryer had broken down so we had clothes hanging on a rope from the living room ceiling. There was trim falling off the wall. Even though my husband was a very gifted carpenter, he couldn't touch it. It was so far down on the priority list that we just pushed a piece a furniture up against it to hold it in place. As I was looking at my surroundings, Kevin barreled in the door with all the might of a papa bear and exclaimed, "I'm hoooome!" Suddenly the floor beneath him gave way, and he fell through—all the way to his chest. It seems that since we never did put a screen door on, our sub-floor slowly weakened from all those Minnesota winters. Since my husband is 6 feet, 3 inches and 245 pounds, he was just the guy to blow a huge hole in our entry- way.

Imagine our little split entry. I am on the couch, arm hanging from the blinds, looking through the clothes. Kevin is standing up to his chest, looking up at me. At once we both busted up laughing. I roared, "We live in the money pit!" It was hilarious. Really, the only options were laughter or crumbling beneath it all. Those lighter moments helped us through the darker ones. I longed to be a "normal" family and I longed to be healed.

He allowed me moments of peace and wonderful words of hope to survive such a dark time—but I really wanted my life back. I saw so many of my friends moving into beautiful homes with lovely decorations. Their children had such nice clothes and they still had money to go out on a date on the weekends. I was beside myself with envy of their situations. I would feel the peace when it was just God and I in my bedroom, but as soon as I saw again how they were living, I wanted to live like that, too. I prayed about it but it would not go away. I was just plain jealous and I couldn't shake it. During a couple of my alone times with God, He moved in my soul and brought me to a deeper place with Him. Here is what I wrote:

5/19/91: "Dear God, my only hope is You. My kidneys have acted up and therefore I have been cut off from my medicine. I have been on one month of IV and have followed that with one and a half months of high doses of oral meds. My body is apparently saying "enough!" Dear God, You are my only hope. The last time I was cut off I became so very sick. I can't bear the thought of going through it all again. In the last three years, I have had two premature labors requiring surgery and bed rest, two very sick children requiring hospitalization, my father's cancer and now Lyme disease. I have been reading the book of Job and have really related to the different phases of his relationship with God. Lord, You have told me that I will be healed. You've made it so clear that even on my worst days, I know it full well. I am struggling with so many things about this. I want it to happen now because I'm so tired of being sick and tired. It's been four years since I have felt normal, and yet I think of all of those who never do get better. I wish they all could. And yet it seems that I have never been more dangerous for God than when I was at the end of myself. And yet I still want to feel good—and I feel guilty for that. God rain down on me. I really feel like You are doing that. Please let it pour. Celebrate with me. I need You so badly. Please pull me all the way out of the pit and lead me on level ground. Put a new song in my heart—a song of praise to my God. Prepare a table for me in the presence of my enemy. Rejoice over me with joy and with life, love and healing. Give me a new song to sing. Lead me in Your higher way. Give me that extra layer of protection that I've lacked all my life. Bring me into a season of rest. Without Your breath, who could stand? Have mercy on me, O Lord, for I take refuge in You. My body and soul depend on You. Let me see Your goodness in the land of the living.

"May Your healing power well up within me and heal all my diseases. Strengthen my frame and give me a new vitality. Without You, I shall go back down into the pit. May Your right hand save me and hold me. May that same right hand cuddle me and nurture me back to health. For my soul trusts in You, O Lord. Dear God, I pray that You fight this battle for me and win it on my behalf, that the righteous may surround me and celebrate Your goodness to me. I love You. Amen."

# CHAPTER SEVENTEEN

# *On Holy Ground*

Warmth, protection and peace had descended upon my bedroom and I barely noticed it. God had graciously spoken through so many people to help me press on. I so appreciated the words of direction and encouragement, yet God still seemed amazingly distant with me personally. I remembered the days when my quiet times involved such intimacy and interaction. Those days seemed so long ago. I wondered how long I would have to wait for the Word of God to come alive to me again, or when I would see things change because I had prayed. That night I laid my head on the pillow and prepared to utter my request for healing for the thousandth time. I admit I may have been lacking a certain expectation. I was so used to throwing up the prayer of instant healing, just to have it drop down on me again. I didn't really expect anything to happen. But it did.

As I prayed, I gazed out the window at the stars in the

moonlight. The Creator of the stars would speak with me that night. Everyone else was sleeping soundly. God was coming down to meet with me and tell me great and wonderful things. He spoke to my heart with loving firmness. I couldn't help but listen. "If I healed you, would you praise Me?"

I blurted out, "'Till the cows come home! I will praise You from the mountaintops! I will tell everyone about it!"

He asked, "Why is that? Is it because I am God, I am on My throne and worthy to be praised? Or simply because you got your way?"

Wow. Below are the journal entry and the poem that came from that blessed time of interaction with my Savior.

5/22/91: "You have shown me great and wonderful things. For the longest time my goal was to be well and comfortable—no matter what. So whenever I wasn't well, my joy went out the window. Then when I got Lyme disease and I was at my sickest, I just wanted to die. Saying that out loud upset Kevin so much, but I couldn't help it. It was how I felt. I felt I'd rather die than live half-way.

"I felt like there was more to life than just surviving … and if I was just surviving, I would rather be with Jesus. I knew in my heart that there was something wrong with this theory.

"Ever since I have been a child, I have been so thankful for the ability to skip, hop, jump and dance—and for the energy to do that. Through life, that had become my highest goal and so whenever illness or injury took that ability from me, my joy left also. Since I have been sick, I've been asking a lot of hard questions such as, 'If I was to get healed today, would I be praising Him because I got my way, or because He is God?' 'Do we say God is good because life is easy, or because He is God?' He is either a loving God or He's not, regardless of good or bad times. 'Is our trust and joy in our gifts or in the Giver of all things?' The reason I've suffered so much disappointment in all of this was because I had the wrong goal. If my goal is health, I will be disappointed. If it is a bigger, better house or an easier life, I will be disappointed. Satan wants us to snatch onto these things so he can pull the rug out from under us. That's why God says 'look to Me and Me alone'—not because He doesn't want us to enjoy good things, but so we don't get let down by the very thing that was meant to be a blessing to us. If He were to send me to a wheelchair, it would be because His plan for me could be accomplished no other way. He may have for me to be a full-time warrior for my kids or husband. How could I choose to die for my comfort and leave soldiers of Jesus here un-prayed for? I can't say that I would happily go to a wheelchair, but I do know now that with my goal as Jesus Christ, I can't be disappointed. For so long I've been fearing the wrong things and taking for granted the important. Heaven is everything and we're down here for such a short time. If we really 'gave' our life to Jesus, was it just to secure our eternity? Is it just a greedy little deal we made with the Father to escape hell? Do we really submit to Him as Lord and King—and turn our lives over to His will and plan for us? If we have given our life to Jesus, it is no longer ours anymore. We must consider that. He is a faithful Father, just because He is.

"Lord, it's been a long three-and-a-half years. Thank You for allowing the pain, the anger and the questions. Thank You that when I was faithless, You were faithful. Thank You for setting me free from myself. You are God and You are so good! I praise You because You are so mighty to save.

"I praise You because You're You. You will never, ever forsake Your own. I love You. "

## *A Time for Everything …*
By Susie Larson

I've walked through many storms,
My prayers were filled with tears.
The enemy was so big,
Confirming all my fears.
To a distant God
I would ever cry,
Just wanting an answer—
Always asking why.
Yet heard I not from Him
Nor His angels singing.
'Twas all that I could do
His robe to keep on clinging.
Then suddenly one night,
As I beckoned Him to be
So real that I could feel Him,
He finally spoke to me.
Said He, "My daughter Susie,
I love you with my life.
No more would I 'er hurt you
Than be the cause of your strife.
You see it's not My hand
That's delivered all this pain.
But it's true My hand is there
To hold yours in the rain.
It's something how I'm 'good'
To those whose life is fair,

And to those whose life is hard,
'I never hear their prayer.'
It's something how men see me
According to their need,
Instead of praise and faith,
They ask and beg and plead.
I am a God who doesn't change with time,
Nor change I with the seasons.
I don't have to explain myself
Nor give you detailed reasons.
I've given all that I could give
When I gave to you My Son.
I emptied out Myself for you
As if you were the only one.
But what I do, I do for you
Because I love you so.
What I allow, I allow for you
Because I want you to grow.
In faith, praise and trust
You will find you are strong
When demands are replaced
By a faith-filled praise song.
It is there you'll find peace
Where there once was strife,
And it will be just enough
To have Me in your life."

I had longed for the Lord to break the sort of "spiritual fast" that I was being forced to walk through, and yet when He finally revealed Himself, I was filled with a holy fear. I lay there in my bed and tore my shirt. God had given me a glimpse of myself. I saw the part of me that sent Him to the cross. I saw how self-absorbed and shallow I was. I realized that He had endured years of selfish prayers and loved me still. I was shaken to my core and realized that my bedroom had become holy ground.

His death and purchase of our souls was so costly and yet we tell Him every day, in many ways, that it just wasn't enough. We want more, we want it now and we want it on our terms. I lay prostrate on my bed in total brokenness. I had somehow forgotten the reason I came to Him that night in the first place. Now all I could think of was to beg for His mercy for the sin in my soul. Nothing was more important than to be one with Him and to live however He asked me to.

My house was falling apart, we were flat broke, and my health was hanging by a thread. But this time instead of feeling sorry for myself, I was feeling very accountable to my Lord—even in the depths of my pain. I was feeling thankful for another chance to love. I found myself asking, "How can I obey You even here? The vats are empty and there is no grain, but I will praise You still. I don't have much to give, but if You can use it, You can have it. Just don't ever leave me and don't let me wander away."

My whole posture towards God had changed.

I didn't think I would ever again shake my fist at God and wonder why He wasn't doing things my way.

I slid out of bed onto my knees and opened my hands in my lap.

*But as for me, I know that my Redeemer lives, and that he will stand upon the earth at last. And after my body has decayed, yet in my body I will see God! I will see him for myself. Yes, I will see him with my own eyes. I am overwhelmed at the thought!* (Job 19:25-27).

# CHAPTER EIGHTEEN

## *Spirit Eyes*

I prayed for the grace to be able to accept my calling in life whatever it would turn out to be. I saw myself in this tunnel of pain that I had been in for so long. Yet instead of running and running through the darkness, trying to find my way out—I found myself sitting down and not being in such a hurry for it all to be over. I wanted to learn everything I could through this experience.

Scripture says that it is better to go to a house of mourning rather than a house where there's a party. When we are in a "party mode," things are not usually in perspective. We tend to throw caution to the wind and enjoy ourselves. On the other hand, when someone we know has experienced an untimely death, we are shocked back into remembering what was so important. Those who work too much suddenly are feeling like staying home more often. Those who snap at their kids feel like being more patient.

Perspective seems to happen when we are rattled into a position that makes us look at life and how we are living it. If there is something in our lives that presses in and reminds us of what is important, then it is a gift from God.

Somewhere in Scripture it reads, "Remember in the darkness what He told you in the light." Isn't it something how God will gloriously speak to us and give us clarity, and yet as soon as the sun drops below the horizon and we can't see clearly with our own eyes, we panic, we grasp and we forget. I was determined not to forget. I would stand up to the enemy of my soul and pray out loud. I would claim the promises of my King and declare that He would again come for me. The more I spoke out loud, the more my faith grew. Somehow I moved from being tossed to and fro by a vicious storm, to being in the eye of it as it swirled around me.

When I finally turned the corner from the hardest part of the sickness, I became more active in life. I taught a few aerobic classes each week, and I was able to care for my boys and clean up after them. I became more involved with women's ministries in our church and so enjoyed that.

All of this was much harder for me to accomplish because I had the ongoing fatigue and joint pain. I did not feel like I was twenty-nine, but I was still glad not to be living my life in my bed, with the ceiling as my view.

I guess my immunities took such a beating, they weren't as efficient as they should have been. For some reason, my endometriosis began to spread and really make me sick. I needed a full hysterectomy to take care of the problem. As I mentioned earlier, we were going to wait five years after our wedding to have children. And yet God had another plan.

I wasn't ready to have children, and yet God knew I had to be. He knew that it was then or never. Never would have devastated me. Here I was five years later, needing a hysterectomy. During that week in the hospital, I kept choking back tears with a heart of thankfulness for my precious little lambs.

How many things do we ask or demand from God that are far from His best for us? It never ceases to amaze me how patiently He endures our selfish little hearts. Every time He takes me to a deeper level, I look back and see the times I really thought I knew what I was talking about. I may have even let pride creep in because I thought I had a grasp of the Creator of the universe. When in truth I held a Dixie cup while the ocean remained. And yet He so sweetly loves, re-directs and loves some more.

CHAPTER NINETEEN

# A Mother's Prayer,
# A Father's Love

or two months we counted the days until we could go to the cabin. This was the resort my parents had taken us every year growing up. My parents, my siblings and all of our children would descend upon this resort like a wave from the ocean. We had many discussions with the kids about the fun they would have and the memories they would make. The morning finally came. We stuffed our minivan full and squashed our three boys in with all the stuff. The kids were so excited they didn't mind a bit. I had put together little surprise packs for each of them to open in the car. They contained things like a new coloring book, ninety-nine-cent sunglasses and a snack.

Once we were on our way, the kids were allowed to open up their packs. They were thrilled. We were on the road about fifteen minutes, (with only four hours and forty-five minutes to go) when Jacob asked, "Are we there yet?"

Only to have little Jordan mimic his big brother by asking, "Der yet?"

Luke, having a real short-term memory problem asked, "Where are we going again?" We just laughed and settled back for a long trip. Every once in a while I would look back at the boys to answer a question, break up a fight or help with a toy.

With every mile north we traveled, Luke developed another red dot on his body. By the time we reached the cabin he had a full case of the chicken pox. It was pouring and continued to do so throughout the next day. I was so disappointed. God knew I desperately needed this vacation. It was costing us a ton of money, most of which we didn't have. I started to imagine being trapped in the cabin for a week and going home exhausted and frustrated.

I instantly felt depressed because my expectations for our first vacation had been dashed. We had prayed hard about going on this vacation and felt that God had said yes to us and that He would provide for our needs. So there we sat with a sick child and pouring rain and I wondered, *Why does it seem that God's plan is designed to confuse us?* It seems that at times we get the opposite of what we think we need most.

Kevin reminded me that we do have a choice in the attitudes we embrace. "Even if it does rain all week, we are still away from home in a cozy cabin. We will have some much-needed time together." I knew he was right and I needed to shake this gloomy mood I had taken on.

Low and behold, after a day and a half of rain, the sun decided to make an occasional appearance through less threatening clouds. We hit the beach to catch a few rays. The next day was also sunny and we enjoyed our time on the beach. I felt a healing take place as I rested on the beach and watched my kids play in the sand. "This is what I'm talking about," I prayed, "Lord, thank You for the sun. It feels so good. And forgive me for doubting Your knowledge of my needs, and even more so of Your loving heart toward those needs. We continually fail to see the bigger picture."

The afternoon came quickly and we gathered our toys from the beach and headed back to the cabin. Jordan was standing on the picnic table bench preparing to step onto the table. Kevin said, "Honey, be careful or you'll fall. " Suddenly Jordan was in a ball under the table holding onto his head. We quickly picked him up and noticed a big gash on the back of his head. My sister Karen, Kevin, Jordan and I headed for the local hospital. Jordan, at two and a half years old, had a will of iron. He thrashed and screamed so hard, they had to put him in a papoose. It was like a straight jacket.

"Mama, hurt! Mama, Daddy, K.K. hurt!" Jordan screamed with terror-filled eyes that asked, "I thought you loved me! How could you be holding me down and let them cause me so much pain?" He screamed and fought for almost an hour. They cut his hair, shaved his head, medicated the wound and stitched him up.

As soon as they unbuckled him from his little prison, he reached for me and buried his sweat-soaked body into my chest. He held me so tight as he rested his head on my shoulder. I just kept telling him how sorry I was that he had to go through it all. Karen, or Auntie K.K. as the kids all called her, stood leaning against the wall of the hospital with tear-filled eyes. We were wiped out. Jordan fell fast asleep during the ride home as we discussed the correlation between our experience and the Father's love.

Being a child of our God in heaven promises that every tear of pain can be coupled with gained wisdom and insight. Sometimes we cry out to God wondering, *Why won't You do something*? He is a God of love and allows many things that are painful, often to save us from a greater evil. Someday Jordan will understand that we had to hold him down while they fixed him up. It was the only way for him to heal.

We ventured out to Lake Vermillion to have some time to heal, make a few memories and enlarge our children's world. We also enlarged their capacity for pain and heartache. We heard in church the other day, "The greater opportunity there is for love, the greater the capacity there is for hate. The greater opportunity for health and healing, the greater possibility there is for sickness and dying." We are given free choice in this world. God has given this to us and is bound by His promise. We have the choice to love, or hate; to look for and search for the good, or dwell on the bad; to humbly accept one another remembering our own imperfections, or to unrealistically expect perfection when we could never be who were asking another to be.

Life is filled with sunny days as well as rainy ones. I continue to be amazed at how big God is and how He consistently teaches us as we go through life. What you look for, you will find. If you're bound and determined to find fault with people and things, you will. If you look for the best, that, too, you will see in time. There is something wrong and something right with almost everything.

*Fix your thoughts on what is true and honorable and right. Think about things that are pure and lovely and admirable. Think about things that are excellent and worthy of praise* (Philippians 4:8).

## CHAPTER TWENTY

# Effects of the Battle

here were so many things I wish we had done differently. We felt as though we were hanging on by a fingernail much of the time. Our priority was survival. I would have liked to pull off "Ward & June Cleaver" household management. I had an ideal of how I wanted things to look and for the life of me, I couldn't pull it off.

As I mentioned earlier, I so envied my friends who lived the "put-together" life. While they were decorating their beautiful homes and planning their next date night, we were talking to bill collectors, nailing trim back to the wall and wondering where it all would take us. My friends tried so hard to encourage me, but still I found myself filled with longing. Somehow, the more the dust settled from the war, the more the damages became apparent. Self-pity found her way into my soul and opened the way for depression to creep in.

The way back seemed like an endless path of almost impossible work. We owed thousands and thousands in medical debt in addition to credit card debt. We had charged items like diapers, formula and medicine. We felt we had no choice at the time. We were simply digging ourselves into a deeper hole. We longed to be debt-free, but had to wonder when that would be. We were only able to pay $5.00 per month to many of our creditors.

I just hated my house. It's hard for me to admit that when there are millions of homeless people, but it still was true. I hated all that it reminded me of. We tried to paint the walls and change the furniture around. We even took down the old pictures that reminded me of my countless months in bed. Nothing seemed to help. I didn't want to live there. I didn't want to be associated with crises and I so desired a change. The time I spent with God continued to bring insight and direction. The struggle was within my own flesh. It was truly something I had to work out.

I couldn't shake the gray cloud that seemed to hang over my head. Still, in the midst of an undiagnosed mild depression, I felt an inner thankfulness that things were better than they ever had been. Things would surely get even better.

We were determined to get our good credit back again. God kept telling us that a mountain can be moved one stone at a time. There is so much in Scripture about trusting the Lord and not tiring in doing what's right. One thing we realized was that we needed to develop a new management style for our lives. Crisis management involves hanging on, reacting to life and putting out fires.

Functional management involves planning, organizing and taking action.

We had spent the last seven years simply responding to everything that was coming our way. So while other couples who were of a similar age, were pretty settled in the way they "did" life, we found ourselves to be babies in this area. We were intelligent, capable people and yet we really needed to re-establish how we did things. It felt a bit like culture shock.

We had our work cut out for us, but we felt so led by God to get back on the path of functional, disciplined living. Another thing we had been sporadic about was our tithing. During the seasons that we faithfully gave, our needs were met. Sometimes our cereal just lasted longer, or I was able to wash more loads than usual. God always kept His promises and He never wavered.

There were those times, though, where our eyes met with the raging waters and we lost sight of our Savior. Any time we clung to the little money we had, it became less in our hands. Whenever we took the few groceries we had and gave some away, things were always okay. God's love never let up even when we had to learn things the hard way. And as soon as we were ready to listen to Him, He was gracious to teach us. I love the verse in Jeremiah that says how the Lord has a wonderful plan for our lives. He wants our best and yet will not move us beyond our capacity to trust and obey.

> *"For I know the plans I have for you," declares the LORD, "plans to prosper you and not to harm you, plans to give you a hope and a future"* (Jeremiah 29:11, NIV).

*Happy are those who are strong in the LORD, who set their minds on a pilgrimage to Jerusalem. When they walk through the Valley of Weeping, it will become a place of refreshing springs, where pools of blessing collect after the rains! They will continue to grow stronger, and each of them will appear before God in Jerusalem.*

*A single day in your courts is better than a thousand anywhere else! I would rather be a gatekeeper in the house of my God than live the good life in the homes of the wicked. For the Lord God is our light and protector. He gives us grace and glory. No good thing will the LORD withhold from those who do what is right. O LORD Almighty, happy are those who trust in you* (Psalm 84:5-7, 10-12).

## Chapter Twenty-One

# *Mountain or Miracle?*

We were busy getting our lives back on track and paying off our bills. I continued to have a nagging, gray feeling, but kept telling myself how good my life was becoming. I still had regular bouts of fatigue and pain, but I was much better off than I had been. Kevin had found a better job and the kids seemed settled.

Luke came down with a virus that wiped him out. He missed a few days of school but couldn't afford to miss much more. He had missed countless days already due to problems with asthma. He was pale and tired but we agreed with his teacher that he needed to be there.

He developed dark circles under his eyes and lumps in his neck, armpits and groin area. It was getting harder and harder for him to wake up in the morning. He just looked bad. When he would brush his teeth, his gums would bleed. One of his legs ached a lot. We obviously had to get him back into the doctor's office. It looked as though he could have leukemia. They needed to play it safe and do all the necessary tests. We once again rallied all the prayer support we could muster. Some people were sick of us by this time, and I can't say I blamed them. I was pretty detached about the whole thing. Some interpreted it as strength; I just think I refused to take it on until I had to. I couldn't borrow the trouble until I knew for sure.

Luke had to be poked and prodded and could not understand why he was at the doctor more often than his two brothers combined. Feeling tired and gray, I went through the motions until I knew for sure what we were dealing with. There was still this overwhelming sense that God was to be revered and praised in all things. I knew that He was on His throne no matter how my life was going. Many who were praying had a bad feeling about Luke's health. These were prayer warriors who had gone to God on our behalf. The tests had been done, and now we would wait and pray.

One morning in the midst of the waiting, my sister called me from her cell phone. She was full of excitement as she began to tell me what the Lord had told her. She said, "You just won't believe what happened! I was driving in to work and praying again for Lukey. Now I'm not one to get pictures and visions from God, but I sure did this time! I saw Lukey standing before our almighty God. The Lord's arms were extended towards Luke. Luke's veins were coming out of his body and running through Jesus' clenched fist. The veins went from Christ's fists back into Luke's body. The blood going up to Jesus was contaminated, but the blood going back into Lukey was purified. I believe the Lord is healing Luke right now!"

## Mountain or Miracle?

As she was telling me this, Luke was making his way up the stairs. (It had been a while since he had gotten up without me waking him up because he was so tired all the time.) He was rubbing his eyes and saying, 'Mommy, I got up all by myself. I think I feel better. I think Jesus is healing me!" This story is almost unbelievable, but it's true. I dropped the phone and ran over to Luke. I swallowed him in my arms and said over and over again, "Oh honey! Thank You, Jesus!" Meanwhile you could hear Karen on the phone shouting, "Hello, hello! Anybody out there?" It was an awesome moment.

That day at school was "Drop Everything and Read" day. Luke got to bring his pillow, sleeping bag and favorite book. When it was time for him to get off the bus, I watched out the window. I had been so protective of him because of his health issues. I watched him step off the bus, arms billowing with a fluffy pillow and sleeping bag. Because he was so top-heavy, he tipped right over and landed face down in the snow.

Right away I wanted to rush to his aid when the Lord whispered in my ear, "Just let him work this out." It was actually pretty comical to see this little boy dressed for winter laying on his rolled up sleeping bag, trying to get the leverage to stand back up.

All of a sudden Luke burst through the door with a huge smile. His arms were flying as he tried to describe his great experience. He proclaimed, "You won't believe what just happened! I came off the bus, I fell over and I didn't know what to do. I reached inside my jacket and grabbed my cross necklace and said, 'O God, just give me the strength to make it home!' and here I am. Isn't that just great? I love it when that stuff happens!" As he went up the stairs with a spring in his step, I looked down at the puddle of winter boots, wet homework and a messed-up sleeping bag—and I smiled.

Luke's tests came back and it turns out that he had a strep virus in his leg. He never had a sore throat during the course of this struggle. It was a most unusual thing. What do you think happened? I guess I will ask Jesus when I get to heaven, after I thank Him for the gift of more time with Luke.

## CHAPTER TWENTY-TWO

# Depression— All in Your Head?

fter everything you have come through and God has done, now you're depressed? Things are finally seeming better in your life!"

I responded to my friend by saying, "I know, I hate this. I want so much to be happy—but I am gray. I have an underlying joy because I know Jesus is intimately involved in our lives, but I just can't shake the feeling of wanting to crawl in bed and pull the covers over my head. I am tired and weary and things feel harder than they should." I decided to talk to a counselor and was prescribed an anti-depressant. I know it's not supposed to work this fast, but on day three I popped out of bed and felt like cleaning my house! I went to counseling once a week and determined to do my part to get out of the pit I was in. I adjusted my diet, made sure I got enough sleep and was careful not to over-commit my time. It wasn't easy, but it was right.

Even though my spiritual life had been transformed, I had a lot to learn about taking my thoughts captive. When I let my thoughts go where my emotions urged them to, it blazed a trail that led me to the dark hole of despair. God showed me that I could not take liberties with thoughts that were destructive to my health. The Bible's promise that God did not give us a spirit of fear but one of power, love and sound mind (2 Tim. 1:7) became a precious promise to me! There was a way out, but only with my cooperation. I started to better identify the times when I was tempted to believe that I was "worthless" because I had produced less. My tendency to go through my days wondering what traumatic thing could be waiting around the corner had to slowly be replaced with trust and hope in my Savior. I struggled with the idea of being on an anti-depressant and yet knew I needed it. I know it is not for everyone struggling through depression, but it was necessary for me.

I had a wonderful counselor who pointed me to Jesus over and over again. I had so much shame for being depressed when my family had waited so long for me to get better. He painted the analogy of healthy, functional people going on trip across the sea. The storms raged and the ship was destroyed. The people hung onto floating pieces of the ship. They hung on for days and days in the freezing ocean until they reached shore. He posed the question, "Would you expect them to hop to their feet and go about their business as if nothing had happened? They would need to be picked up off the shore and brought to the hospital. They would need fluids, rest and little bits of food at a time. It would take enough good days to bring healing from all of those terrible days at sea. You have nothing to be ashamed of and a lot to be proud of. You are

114

still married! I don't know many that would have come out of this in one piece. You have had a series of overlapping, unresolved crises that you've never had a chance to sort through let alone bring closure to. One wasn't even over before the next one started. It's just going to take time to heal."

It felt like he tossed me a rope that would help pull me up to a level path. One of the biggest things he did for me was to hold me accountable to doing nice things for myself. He would ask me, "What have you done for yourself this week?"

I would proudly answer, "I went to the bathroom by myself, no kids!" Over time I learned to treat myself to little things that were just for me. A scented candle, a magazine, a bubble bath. These things had a very healing effect on me. I meditated on Scripture about joy, life and being transformed by changing the way I think.

Working through depression is quite a task, especially in the Christian community. There are many who have no mercy for those going through such a thing. If a person has not been affected by it in one way or another, it is easy for them to "sum up" the depressed person and label them as less than. The worst thing you can do to a depressed person is to heap another weight on their shoulders by telling them it's just a mind over matter situation. My counselor wisely asked me once, "What do you do when Luke has an asthma attack? Do you tell him if he would just think positive, he could breathe better?" Yikes.

There are chemicals in the brain that sometimes need assistance in being regulated. While it is true that much relies on how we manage our depression, it is important to understand it is a sickness that needs to be treated. People who are critical or self-righteous are lethal to a depressed person. It is important to surround yourself with gracious, loving people who will walk with you through this kind of thing. I went to counseling and took the medication for one year. I slowly decreased my medicine until I was free of it. I am thankful for the experience because I have so much compassion for those who are walking the same path. I have learned what my "triggers" are and I am careful to manage things accordingly.

One day as I was praying and looking out the window, I noticed a huge oak tree stretching toward the sky. Its roots were bulging out of the ground but went deep down into the earth. Staying power. That's what that tree had. It had been there a long time, through a lot of different weather. I wanted that for our lives. I wanted roots, consistency and a sense that we weren't going anywhere. The years past were filled with anything but predictability.

Journal entry 5/11: "It has been a long, cold winter. We have had six months filled with more gray, chilly days than not. This past week, spring in its beautiful way, quenched the dark clouds of winter. Windows were opened, music was turned up and people came out of hiding. There was a huge sigh of relief in the air. The time for re-planting and restoration had come!

"Today a cold wind blows through town, preparing the way for an unwelcome snowstorm. Many become angry, shaking their fists at the sky—as if their tiny little limb could stop one snowflake from falling. The cheerful smiles are replaced with an expression of someone who's been tricked. Some think it would have been easier to never have tasted that touch of spring, than to have enjoyed it for one moment, and lose it the next.

"Others, though, have seen this kind of thing before. Seasons change.

"After the rain, the rainbow appears. Healing comes. Restoration is on the horizon. If we become still and quiet, we can hear the birds singing, as they have done all week. And if we can boldly look up into the clouds, we will eventually see hints of the blue, majestic sky. A sky that is still very much in place.

"The springtime healing is not the illusion, this little storm is.

"Spring is here and things *have* changed. We are not where we were even a month ago. Seasons change, circumstances change and even hearts, if we let them, will change. The Word of God says that if we go into the stormy times carrying seeds to sow, we shall come through carrying bundles in our arm. (Psalm 126:5-6, NIV)."

My paraphrase is this: *If* we go into hard seasons of life carrying our tiny seed of faith—the faith that says everything else has gone cold, we shall find our God in this somehow—we *will* come through the hard times having found Him abundantly. When God opens the skies and provides a brief moment of relief from our circumstances, is this a cruel joke to tease and reminds us how tough things really are? No! I submit that it's a precious gift from a patient Father who wishes we were not so earth-bound. Since we are, though, He provides us with an occasional visual aid that tells us, "Things really are changing and I am busy and active in your life. Take these moments as a foretaste of my gifts to you. Don't be fooled by the enemy's attempt to re-create the season you have just come from. Do the trees bud in the winter? Do the birds sing together so sweetly in January? Could you see with

Spirit-eyes like you do now, even a year ago? Things have changed and continue to do so. Let go of doubt, anger and your 'rights' and hold fast to the tiny seed of hope that reminds you that I am God, I am in control, I love you deeply, I am aware of the clouds, but I also see the blue that hasn't gone anywhere. I am motivated by love and My eye is on you. Let go of your useless baggage, but don't let go of your seed, for soon it will produce a beautiful garden."

Yes, spring is here and we can know that this storm too, shall pass.

## CHAPTER TWENTY-THREE

# *Home Sweet Home!*

second job, a lot of praying and help from friends allowed us to build ourselves a home. I had prayed in such detail about the place where we would place our roots in the ground. I prayed for trees, lots of trees, cool neighbors, great schools and lots of kids. All of these things became our reality as we moved into the house the Lord provided. Our closing day arrived and after signing all the papers, we headed out the door. We were holding hands and swinging them back and forth like teenagers. As soon as we exited the building I jumped up and down and shouted at the top of my lungs. I jumped up and wrapped my arms and legs around my husband in broad daylight. Distinguished-looking people walked by us and entered the building. I didn't care, I was blessed, restored and in love.

We went to pick up our boys and bring them to our new place. They blew in the door and ran from one room to the next. "Is it really ours, do we have to give it back? Can we stay here tonight without the furniture?" I clasped my hands close to my heart and spilled over with joy as I watched them thoroughly take in this place that they would call home.

After a long day of moving boxes and furniture, friends and family headed home. Our bedrooms were not yet put together, so we all camped out in our bedroom with sleeping bags, pillows and a bowl of popcorn. We all lay on our stomachs in a circle facing each other. We giggled with excitement as we talked about this new stage of life. Kevin quieted us all down and had something to say. "Boys, you know Daddy has not been home much because I have been working two jobs to help get us here. But it's important that you know that it's not because of me that we get to have this house. This home was provided by our God in heaven. He is the one who decided to restore us and bless us in this way. We can't let one night pass without bowing our heads and giving Him thanks for all He has done."

Our boys instantly folded their hands and bowed their heads. As I bowed my head, I was hit all of a sudden with a flood of emotion. This moment represented so much to me. I had hung on and dreamed of the day when the season would change in my life. I had waited, watched and hoped for restoration. God had given me permission to believe Him for a new place, a new season and a new start. The Lord whispered into my ear, "It's a big deal when My children trust Me with their pain. It's not a small thing at all. I am a rewarder of those who seek after Me."

I lost it right then and there. I cried loud sobs and there was no stopping me. Jordan turned to his daddy and asked, "Is Mommy sad?"

Still looking at me he responded, "No, Son, she is very, very glad."

*I waited patiently for the* LORD *to help me, and he turned to me and heard my cry. He lifted me out of the pit of despair, out of the mud and mire. He set my feet on solid ground and steadied me as I walked along. He has given me a new song to sing, a hymn of praise to our God. Many will see what he has done and be astounded. They will put their trust in the* LORD. *Oh, the joys of those who trust the* LORD, *who have no confidence in the proud, or in those who worship idols. O* LORD *my God, you have done many miracles for us. Your plans for us are too numerous to list. If I tried to recite all your wonderful deeds, I would never come to the end of them* (Psalm 40:1-5).

LORD, *you alone are my inheritance, my cup of blessing. You guard all that is mine. The land you have given me is a pleasant land. What a wonderful inheritance! I will bless the* LORD *who guides me; even at night my heart instructs me. I know the* LORD *is always with me. I will not be shaken, for he is right beside me. No wonder my heart is filled with joy, and my mouth shouts his praises! My body rests in safety* (Psalm 16:5-9).

## CHAPTER TWENTY-FOUR

# *All Other Ground is Sinking Sand*

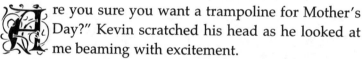

re you sure you want a trampoline for Mother's Day?" Kevin scratched his head as he looked at me beaming with excitement.

"I'm sure! It will be so fun! We'll be one happy, hopping, bouncing family!" We jumped to our heart's content. It was such a treat and lent itself to many family fun nights. Several feet away, Kevin put in a fire pit for bonfires. We just loved sitting out there roasting marshmallows, making S'mores and watching the sunset.

Every morning I would wake up and look out my bedroom window. "Thank You, Lord. Thank You so much for the trees and for this place and for your healing hand in my life." I would go down to the kitchen, pour myself a cup of coffee and sit down with my Bible and journal. Verse after verse came to life and jumped off the page at me! I would sometimes sit for two hours straight—just reading, writing, praying and saying "thanks." This was just the opposite of those desert times of hanging on by a fingernail.

When I would pray, things would change. When I would talk to God, I would sense His presence and hear His voice. I enjoyed an intimacy unlike anything I ever had before. I no longer felt like I was "open game" for the enemy of my soul. I felt wrapped in the arms of God and protected by His fierce and strong angels. The wind had shifted in my life and the sky was blue once again.

"I hurt my neck. I fell off the tramp," Jordan complained as he came in with his filthy hands wrapped around his neck. He walked into my bedroom and started to scream. He collapsed into my arms as I slowly lowered him to the ground. We ended up lying on the floor between the bed and the wall. "Don't breathe, Mama, it hurts when your chest moves." I was trying to get Jake or Luke's attention but every time I took in a breath before speaking, he would wince and cry harder. We lay there for the longest time.

Luke was out riding his bike when Keith, our neighbor, asked how he was doing today. "Fine, but I think my brother broke his neck."

He pedaled away and Keith shouted, "Wait a minute, where is he?"

"I think he's in the house with my mom." Nothing like making a mountain into a mole hill.

Thankfully, Keith found his way into our home and looked for us. Every time he would call out for us I would want to respond but Jordan begged me not to move. I looked up to see our new neighbor looking down at me with a very concerned look on his face. I so wanted to re-invent myself so my new neighbors wouldn't associate us with crises. Our lawn wasn't even in and here I was, waving good-bye to my new neighbors through the back window of the ambulance. Oh well....

Jordan screamed at the top of his lungs every time they tried to move him for x-rays. He had a very bad sprain and strain and needed to wear a cervical collar.

He loved that thing. He got more attention than he knew what to do with. We were very fortunate that it turned out the way it did. It was time for some serious tramp rules. One morning about two weeks after this little event, Jordan woke up with a plum-sized lump in his neck. I took him to the doctor thinking it was a muscle spasm from the tramp accident. The doctor inquired about other symptoms and I remembered the night sweats Jordan had been having lately. He would crawl into bed with us at night and his shirt would be soaked. I am a basically intelligent person, and I have been through enough health stuff to be able to put two and two together, but somehow I missed this one. The doctor ran a few tests and told us he would call us.

Shortly after we arrived home, we received a call from a large hospital that specializes in care for children. They requested that we come down. We packed up the family and headed back out again. We approached the registration desk and checked in. After taking our names, the registrar sent for the person who was waiting for us. We were escorted to the elevator and got off on the children's oncology floor. We all looked around wondering what we were doing there.

A nice young man greeted us and began to give us the tour. "This is where you can eat your meals, and this is where your family can stay if they come to visit. You can do your laundry here any time you need to." This is a wonderful hospital and they do wonderful things for children. We were so impressed with the proficiency in which they operated. They were like clockwork with the way they helped you adjust to your new surroundings. In our case, there was a little glitch because we were not sure why we were there. Still we felt that if you are going to go through such a thing, this is the place to be. When we got to the room where Jordan would stay, the doctor was waiting for us.

He was so wonderful, so kind and so apologetic. He explained the gap in communication and felt terrible for it. "Jordan has symptoms that are very classic of Burketts Lymphoma. Kids with this disease have a large lump and night sweats but are otherwise completely normal by day." Kevin and I sat next to each other on Jordan's bed. He was already playing in the playroom with his new friends, many of whom had no hair.

He explained the further tests that would be needed. Some tests looked bad, others more hopeful. The doctor described chemotherapy and needed to inform us of this possibility. As soon as he left us, Kevin said, "I will shave my head so it won't be so hard for Jordan. We will get through this together. I know it will be okay." I knew it would be, too. We were in a bit of shock but it wasn't like before. Crises in the past had rocked my world and shaken me to the core.

It was a blessing that Jordan landed in soft sand. It was a bigger blessing though, that our lives were not built on the shifting sand of circumstance. This time our hope and sure foundation were in Jesus Christ our Lord. We knew

Him to be so faithful to His children and He would never forsake His own. I was very sober in spirit, but I didn't have that deep fear that was once so familiar to me. I had spent the past seven years shifting my hope and trust from the things of this world to the things of God. It was so comforting to have that settled when something like this was about to touch one of our most prized possessions.

"What does obedience look like here, Lord?" I prayed as I sat in a rocker and watched Jordan play.

"Watch the other moms and dads. Look at the fatigue in their eyes and pray for them. They live this every day. Listen to them and help to carry their loads." I looked around at some of the world's greatest unsung heroes. Life moves so fast: appointments, luncheons, hockey games, videos, late fees, highways, skyways, hallways, my way. Here it was just the opposite. Aches, pains, prayers, tears, hallways, dark ways, lost ways, slow days, not my way. Wow. Nobody looked polished around here. They looked tired and weary. They didn't seem to notice because it was not their focus—their children were. They shared their stories and I lost track of time. I was thankful to pray for a grandmother and was blessed to receive comfort from her as well. I had an underlying strength in this that held fast. This was a powerful revelation to me.

*God is our refuge and strength, always ready to help in times of trouble. So we will not fear, even if earthquakes come and the mountains crumble into the sea. Let the oceans roar and foam. Let the mountains tremble as the waters surge! A river brings joy to the city of our God, the sacred home of the Most High. God himself lives in that city; it cannot be destroyed. God will protect it at the break of day. The nations are in an uproar, and kingdoms crumble! God thunders, and the earth melts! The* LORD *Almighty is here among us; the God of Israel is our fortress* (Psalm 46:1-7).

## CHAPTER TWENTY-FIVE

# *In the Garden*

ournal entry 1/20/97, *an imaginative portrayal of a meeting with Jesus*: "As I enter the beautiful garden, I pray that my Lord will show up. There were so many times I thought He would not show, so I just walked past the garden, unaware that my decision ensured my missing Him.

"The sun is shining perfectly and reflects the flowers in their best light. I am wearing a sundress and walking barefoot through the garden. Everything is peaceful and wonderful. I am in awe of His creation of beauty. And to think—the One who created all of this loves me even more! Could it really be? Could my Jesus really love me that much?

"'Yes, I do, more than you'll ever know.'

"I turn to see my Savior—face to face. He is beautiful

and simple. He is strong and tender. He is larger than life and yet He's real right here, right now. Before I am able to get a word out, Jesus kneels down to wash my feet. I feel a little awkward, but mostly I feel love. It is something how my King is such a servant. More than anything, I want to be like Him.

"I am no longer self-conscious. I am absorbed with only Jesus. After He washes my feet, He sits down and looks into my eyes. He then says so sweetly, 'I know of your pain and your fear. I am aware of all that concerns you. It broke My heart when you struggled through those desert times and yet it was those very times that strengthened you for My service. You were becoming a lean soldier for My cause. You learned how to use the armor I have given you. I am proud of you. I delight in you and I expect great things from you. I do not expect perfection, so you shouldn't either. I do however, expect you to run the race as to win the prize. In this life, there will be a lot of baggage that will seek to be carried by you. Heavy weights such as pride, unforgiveness, jealousy, doubt and anxiety. You must refuse these and if you forget everything else, remember to love and to forgive. You will be fighting a losing battle without the supernatural power of My love and forgiveness. Embrace them—even if they cost you everything. I will be right here within you. I whisper, so you must take time to listen.'

"For a moment, I could say nothing. He answered many of my questions before I could ask them. 'Jesus,' I said, 'how can I be sure not to lose sight of everything You are teaching me?'

"He smiled and replied, 'You must look for Me in all things. Wisdom can be gained in the most menial tasks.

## In the Garden

You must keep your belt of truth on, stay in the Word and learn from it. Love and encourage each other, remind yourselves what Eternity will be like. When you look at each other, see Me and respond accordingly. Satan has set many traps for the believer. One of them is to feel justified in tearing one another down for whatever reason. Satan laughs and My love is mocked when Christians treat each other this way. This cannot be! Again, your greatest weapons against pain, fear and rejection are faith, hope, love and forgiveness. Your only hope for survival and the greatest thing you can do with your day, or with your moment, is simply to love, just as I have loved you.'

"I sat on the ground with my head resting in His lap. He stroked my head and assured me all was well. I closed my eyes and embraced the moment. When I opened them again, I found myself leaning against a big rock. I could no longer see Him, but I knew He was with me. I would follow Him all the days of my life."

*Who shall separate us from the love of Christ? Shall trouble or hardship or persecution or famine or naked-ness or danger or sword? As it is written: "For your sake we face death all day long; we are considered as sheep to be slaughtered." No, in all these things we are more than conquerors through him who loved us. For I am convinced that neither death nor life, neither angels nor demons, neither the present nor the future, nor any powers, neither height nor depth, nor anything else in all creation, will be able to separate us from the love of God that is in Jesus Christ our Lord* (Romans 8:35-39, NIV).

*Now you have every spiritual gift you need as you eagerly wait for the return of our Lord Jesus Christ. He will keep you strong right up to the end, and he will keep you free from all blame on the great day when our Lord Jesus Christ returns. God will surely do this for you, for he always does just what he says, and he is the one who invited you into this wonderful friendship with his Son, Jesus Christ our Lord* (1 Corinthians 1:7-9).

## CHAPTER TWENTY-SIX

# *River of Love*

ournal entry 8/4/99: "The other night as I lay in bed, tossing and turning, I began to pray fervently. Somewhere between wakefulness and sleep I saw this vision and prayed this prayer. I was at the base of a steep hill. A river ran down it and seemed to go on forever. The river was blood red. As I started my journey, I began with my earliest memory of sin. I confessed the sin in detail, then I knelt down and rolled this old baggage into the river of blood. I said, 'I bury this sin in the blood of the Lamb and receive His full and perfect forgiveness.'

"I rose to my feet but didn't have to walk far to come to my next memory. I confessed it in detail, looked into my Shepherd's eyes and said, 'I really am so sorry' He smiled gently and nodded toward the river. I knelt down and rolled the next baggage, which was heavier, into the river of blood. I watched the current go down hill, but could see no signs of my old baggage.

"This journey lasted throughout the night. Each and every memory of my sin was recognized, identified and buried in the river of love. My Lord gently helped me to remember everything I needed to. He allowed me to do the work of rolling them into the river, and yet in an instant the river enveloped the baggage.

"My work, the work of confession and repentance was small in comparison to His work of supplying the blood for the river of love. His work cost Him everything and He knew it would. He shed His blood, because He is love. And though my work of repentance is small in comparison, it is extremely significant. For if the baggage is allowed to accumulate by the riverside, I have, by my lack of action, allowed a dam to be built between my Savior and myself. Oh that nothing would come between my Savior and me! Even though (to my memory) I had already been confessing sin throughout my Christian life, the Lord knew that the enemy of my soul had been pressing in and accusing me. For Jesus to take me back as far as I could remember, and allow me to see my sin swallowed up by victory, was a cleansing and secure reminder of what He had done for me. My victory has been won through Jesus Christ, God's son!"

*If we say we have no sin, we are only fooling ourselves and refusing to accept the truth. But if we confess our sins to him, he is faithful and just to forgive us and to cleanse us from every wrong* (1 John 1:8-9).

## CHAPTER TWENTY-SEVEN

# *What We Really Need*

We have great news and we owe you an apology." We stood in the doorway of Jordan's hospital room. The doctor was glad to inform us that our son had mononucleosis. We looked down the hall to see Jordan chasing a pedal racecar around the nurses' station. It's driver giggled with excitement. He was a sweet child with a rare form of cancer. He had no hair and a great laugh. Mononucleosis? We looked at our high-energy child and wondered what part of him was tired. The doctor, agreeing, said he displayed no signs of fatigue, sore throat or the countless other symptoms associated with this common illness. He apologized for being so quick to inform us of the possible cancer and yet explained how much his symptoms paralleled that of Burketts Lymphoma. We didn't at all feel that he owed us an apology.

We were so impressed with how thorough they were in their care for these children.

We believe it is utterly possible that the healing hand of God touched Jordan. We will not know for sure until we see Him on the other side, but we do know what mono looks like and that Jordan never had those symptoms before, during or after this ordeal. We packed up Jordan's bag and said good-bye to the few friends we had made. We drove home so full of thanks for our outcome and yet so painfully aware of those we left behind. They had to stay, they had to wait, and they had to walk a path they hadn't signed up for. I couldn't get them out of my mind. As happy as I was to be in a new place, and beginning a new season, I could clearly see that I wasn't being blessed just for my comfort.

Life is such a precious gift. When we are weak, we need gracious people around us to help us along. We don't need those who wonder why we can't get it together or those who breathe a heavy sigh when they hear we are not better yet. We need love and patience. When we are strong, we need to offer that hand to the weak. We must not think that things are good for us because we are good. Things are good because God is good and He has given us a break from having to look at ourselves for a time. We need each other and we deeply need God.

> *Now you can have sincere love for each other as brothers and sisters because you were cleansed from your sins when you accepted the truth of the Good News. So see to it that you really do love each other intensely with all your hearts* (1 Peter 1:22).

Now that you can, see that you do.

## CHAPTER TWENTY-EIGHT

# My Vulnerable Love

Broad-shouldered, sure-footed, hard-working, kind and gentle. These are some of the words that describe my husband. I am sure that I have made him sound almost perfect even though that would be impossible. He is the most wonderful man I know. He has his faults as we all do, but his strengths far out-weigh anything else. He carried most of the physical burden during our years in the wilderness and did so with such kindness and grace. Long after we had come out of the darkest of times, he was still forging ahead at a bull's pace.

He would blaze through the door after a long day of work with such focus he didn't realize how fast he was still moving. He would whip through the pile of mail and listen to the kid's stories with partial attention. It seemed to take him longer and longer each night to relax and

**137**

unwind. I began to ask God to bring him to a place of balance and peace.

His job was so extremely demanding and his work ethic was equally as intense. He had huge responsibilities and it wasn't like he could just let go and relax. I longed for him to have more of a margin, but his job showed no signs of letting up. He had become so used to carrying the world on his shoulders, it seemed unnatural to do anything else.

The holidays approached and I looked forward to some much-needed family time. We had so much fun putting up our tree and decorating it to Alvin and the Chipmunks. I baked cookies and reveled in the newness of my life. I found myself thanking God every time I had a free moment. As I sat down to write our Christmas letter, Kevin expressed the desire to do it himself. This was unusual for our house. We had our roles. He built things, and I wrote things. I loved the idea and told him to go for it.

He wrote a most beautiful letter. He expressed our love and gratitude for the family and friends who meant so much to us. He thanked them for hanging in there with us when it would have been easier to go away. He gave God the credit for getting us through a long journey. With a happy update of our family life, he wished everyone a blessed holiday.

Kevin's family arrived on Christmas day. We had one of our best Christmases ever! We shared a delightful meal and we made gingerbread houses. (Being the contractors that they are, Kevin and his twin brother, Keith, built commercial gingerbread buildings. They even satisfied the city code!) We opened gifts as we listened to Christmas music. We then turned all the lights down except the tree. We lit a candle and shared what God had done in our lives over the past year. One by one, we lit another candle and heard another story of the things God had been doing. Finally the room was illuminated with candlelight and we sang, "O Come Let Us Adore Him." It was a blessed event.

That night, as family filed out the door, we padded up the stairs and collapsed in bed. We snuggled and recalled the memories we had just made. It was that night we discovered a lump on Kevin that had not previously been there. He minimized it, but I called the doctor the next day. They wanted to see him right away.

As we waited in the doctor's office, we made small talk. When the doctor came in, he reassured us that many such lumps are simply fluid-filled sacs and nothing to worry about. "The ones to worry about are solid and attached." The doctor explained as he asked Kevin to change. After the examination, he turned to us and said, "Well this one feels solid and attached."

I just knew this was a bad situation and I could feel the ache well up from the deepest part of my gut. It looked as though Kevin could have testicular cancer. We heard countless stories of men who had this and suffered very little. It is such a treatable form of cancer that if it's caught early, prognosis is very good.

Over the course of the following days, more tests would be scheduled. When Kevin wasn't around, I would sob and pray. I couldn't explain why I felt such a deep ache. I just knew things wouldn't be as simple for Kevin as they had for the others we had heard about.

After the scans were taken, we were to wait a week before we could see the urologist. By this time I had it resolved in my mind that this could be bad, but we would get through it. Kevin was still in the stage of thinking he could muscle his way through this like he had everything else. You can't really blame him. He was never sick— always strong and very capable.

We made arrangements for our kids and drove to the professional building across from the hospital. We waited to meet the urologist. When they called our names, we found our places in a little room. The doctor came in, introduced himself and put the film up on the lighted board. "Oh my," he said. It was his first time to look at them. I instantly saw the outline of what he was worried about. The doctor spun around on his chair and faced my husband.

"We are looking at about a year's worth of growth here. We will have to send you to the hospital for blood tests but this is most definitely what cancer looks like."

The tumor filled the testicle and had tentacles that stretched up toward his stomach. I watched Kevin receive this news with beads of sweat escaping from his forehead. His face was reddened with the pain of hearing what was going to be done to him. "We will need to do a cut about this long." He held his hands up to show us a length that made us both swallow hard.

"If it's Seminoma cancer, you will require radiation, if it's Non-Seminoma you will need chemotherapy. If the cancer has spread to your stomach, you may need a portion of your stomach removed." The doctor was very competent and very clinical in his descriptions of the potential treatments. Kevin sat there until the doctor excused himself to see his next patient. We exited the building and looked across the parking lot at the hospital. It was a beautiful winter night. Snowflakes were falling slowly and softly. The sky was dark with bright, distinct stars. We held hands, walked slowly and prayed. We thanked God for all

He had done in our lives. We thanked Him for our families, our friends and for the love we shared. We thanked Him ahead of time for the outcome of this crisis. We declared His faithfulness and determined to lean on Him.

*I will praise the LORD at all times. I will constantly speak his praises. I will boast only in the LORD; let all who are discouraged take heart. Come, let us tell of the LORD's greatness; let us exalt his name together. I prayed to the LORD, and he answered me, freeing me from all my fears. Those who look to him for help will be radiant with joy; no shadow of shame will darken their faces. I cried out to the LORD in my suffering, and he heard me. He set me free from all my fears. For the angel of the LORD guards all who fear him, and he rescues them. Taste and see that the LORD is good. Oh, the joys of those who trust in him! Let the LORD's people show him reverence, for those who honor him will have all they need. Even strong young lions sometimes go hungry, but those who trust in the LORD will never lack any good thing* (Psalm 34:1-10).

## CHAPTER TWENTY-NINE

# *Persistent Prayer*

s Daddy gonna die?" Jordan asked as we cleaned the bathroom together. I stopped what I was doing instantly so I could focus on him. He didn't want to stop cleaning to look up at me. He feverishly scrubbed the tub as he waited for my answer.

"No, honey, Daddy is going to be sick for a while but I just know he will be fine." It appeared that he hadn't heard a word I said because before I could say any more he blurted out, "'Cuz that's all I think about all day, and all night, if Daddy's gonna die. Well that ... and Nutty Bars 'cuz they sell 'em on the treat cart at school now!" Kevin was quite pumped to be up there with Nutty Bars.

The surgery was major and the recovery was equally so. It seems the bigger they are, the harder they fall. Kevin rested in his favorite easy chair covered with a blanket. We had many wonderful people come to visit. I looked at him and was more determined than ever to see him get to a place of balance and rest. I began to intercede for him intensely. I went before God and prayed, "Dear Lord, I just know that You care deeply for the family. You care when we are too busy and You love it when our priorities are in order. I ask You to do Your great work and move things around in Kevin's life. He has been such a wonderful father and husband. He has carried so much of the burden. Now I believe it is time for him to remember that he is Your child first and foremost. Help him to rest in You. Help him to find a job that allows him to go on field trips with our boys once in a while. If we have to take a major cut in pay, give us the grace to do that, but I pray that he would be in a job that doesn't move at such a relentless pace. Your word says Your yoke is easy and Your burden is light. You own the cattle on a thousand hills, it is nothing for You to move heaven and earth to get him to a place of balance. I know this is Your will and so I pray it in the name and authority of Jesus Christ, my Lord. Amen."

> *And we can be confident that he will listen to us whenever we ask him for anything in line with his will. And if we know he is listening when we make our requests, we can **be sure** that he will give us what we ask for* (1 John 5:14-15, emphasis mine).

I went boldly before the throne of grace (Hebrews 4:16) and called on God's great power. I prayed with all the persistence and focus I had in me. I constantly submitted myself to God's authority and will, and then I prayed—hard.

In my quiet times I pray, read and journal. Many years ago I felt impressed by the Lord to include listening prayer. (There is a book out with this title but it is somewhat different than what I am talking about.) There were times when I sensed God had something to say to me. I would write down those thoughts as clearly as I could. Sometimes the words had no impact on me, but later I would find they blessed someone else. During the course of Kevin's cancer, I recorded one such prayer.

Journal entry 2/5/98: "Listen to me, young man. I have redeemed you and I work daily to perfect you for the day of your homecoming with Me. You are a brilliant, special child of God. I have bestowed upon you unusual gifts of strength and perspective. You have thought at times that these were yours to own. They have nothing to do with you but everything to do with My purpose in you.

"Never think for a moment that you have ownership of these attributes lest the enemy sneak in and build a fortress of pride and subtle arrogance. You are a warrior for My cause and you have incredible character. I give you one command and one focus—love the Lord your God with all your heart soul and might, and love your neighbor as yourself. Are you doing that right now? Or are you running the race that the world has signed you up for?

"Are you exceeding the expectations of the wrong people? Make no mistake about it, when you please Me, you will disappoint others at times. You have to make a choice for the things I cherish or they will be snatched from you. You are an everlasting joy to Me. You are My son and I love you so very much. I have much that I want to teach you and I want to re-direct you. In order for Me to teach you, you must become a student.

"Are you willing to sit under My authority no matter what it may cost you? Be assured that I know the pain and heartache you have been through and I know where the locust has eaten. I have restored and blessed you because I love you. I have firmed up in you your staying power, your perspective and your patience. Now I want to shake in you your strong, earthly strength and self-reliance.

"I know that you mean well, but it will kill you in the end if you don't lay down your play toys and pick up my real weapons of the Spirit. Trade in the things that have worked for you up until now and receive a new map, a new set of circumstances and a new level of trust. Trust Me, My son. I will take you to a new level of depth with your Savior. I will provide for you and I will require your trust and faith in Me, not yourself.

"You will love the journey once you are on it. It's the getting there that will scare you. Don't let the enemy fool you. The place I am taking you is to the center of My will. You will reach for Me more often. You will smile, relax and play more. You will see more of your family and reckon with the forces of evil. You will do all of this because I have invested in you and I love you.

"You will know that I am in charge and will suddenly feel relieved instead of pressured. You will give grace to those who need grace and you will listen more. You will forgive more and you will feel more. You will walk closer to the heartbeat of God than you ever have. You will forget the pain of your youth and will stand tall as a man and warrior for My kingdom.

"Every day I will point you in the direction you are to go. Some days will require that you just listen, other days will require baby steps of trust. Each new day those levels will grow. You will see My hand in it no matter what man may say. You will know that you and I are having a one-on-one conversation from heaven to earth. No one else needs to understand. You will. I will lead, you will follow. Spring is coming. Amen."

## CHAPTER THIRTY

# A Different View

As much as we all loved him, Kevin walked a lonely path that took him deep within himself. The radiation made his stomach and spinal cord swell. Then anti-nausea medicine caused his jaw to lock up at night. He moved slower, said little and leaned on things a lot. It was almost too much for me to take to see my big, strong husband walk through such a trial. As he reclined in his chair with eyes closed, listening to Christian music, I knew he was having his own time with God.

He still managed to work a few hours most days. This gave him the fighting spirit he needed. I don't know that he accomplished much but it didn't matter. One day he came home from radiation looking ready for bed. He came to the kitchen and leaned on the counter. "What are we doing?" he asked. I let him finish. "On my way home today there was a back-up of traffic on the entrance ramp to the highway. Everyone was honking at this one pokey car and some even honked and gestured as they drove around him. I was too tired to do anything but wait my turn. When I pulled up next to the car that was slowing everything down, I almost died. It was one of my radiation buddies. He has lung cancer and he doesn't have long. He was coughing and coughing, that's why he wasn't driving. I would have been one of those people rushing around him to get to my next appointment, never thinking what that person may be walking through. I have been moving so fast that it has seemed impossible to slow down. I can't believe that God loves me so much that He would slow me down before my kids were all grown and gone."

I sat on the counter with my hand over my mouth in effort to keep my composure. He walked over to me and put his head into my chest and we just cried together. If I had held him any tighter, I would have hurt him. There in our kitchen, we held each other for a very long time.

Here is the letter that Kevin sent out to everyone:

"To all who prayed for me,

"I am not sure where to start. First I need to explain this letter. In the last three months, I have received a grocery bag full of cards and letters. Many days I had up to thirty calls. I have heard about numerous prayer chains praying for my family and me. We have eaten meals prepared by some people we hardly know. I have had the urge to call every person who has done any of these things for me, but I was too sick and just didn't have the energy to spend. I can't even begin to thank every one of you for all you have done for us. I am humbled and amazed at how the family of God takes care of it's own. My life has been changed as a result of this difficult time. I wouldn't wish this on anyone, but I wouldn't trade it either. I watched God change my heart, my attitudes and my priorities. I needed a way to respond to all of you. I hope this letter does not seem impersonal—it is extremely personal to me.

"After being told I had testicular cancer at Christmas time, my world changed. I have dealt with difficult health issues with Susie and the kids, but never from this side. This time it was me and I didn't know how to handle it very well. I haven't seen so many different doctors or had so many tests in my whole life. I had surgery to remove a tumor on January 13 and, after my recovery, radiation treatments five days a week. I felt myself getting sicker and weaker as each week passed. Those of you who know me know that I am much better at being the caretaker than the 'caretakee.' I laid in a chair or in bed from the time I got home from radiation treatment until the next morning. This was very hard for me, but every day I had a handful of cards and phone messages, some of which I played over and over. I felt so prayed-over, I can't describe it. One thing I am so thankful for is that God never left me alone. In fact, I have never felt God's presence more than I have in the last three months. I am convinced that all your prayers moved the heart of God on my behalf.

"He has stayed very close to me. Each day after working a couple hours (normal daily life) I would go to radiation therapy (where everyone has cancer). Sometimes making that transition was very hard. The conversations I had with the people in the waiting room were amazing. We were all there for the same thing. We were all scared. None of us wanted to be there. All of what was important to us was being changed in varying degrees. Sometimes I think God puts us on our back to make us look up at Him. I am slowly getting better and prognosis is good. I will need to go through all the same initial tests again every six months for a while. I know that many of you have very similar things you have dealt with and your help and understanding has been greatly appreciated. Please continue to pray for me as I recover and that my treatment works. Also, please pray against fear of returning cancer. I will need God to keep reminding me that He is in control and I will need to let Him be. All of you, by your prayers, made this difficult time bearable for me. I thank you all from the deepest part of my heart. You are good friends.

"I love you all.

"Kevin."

## CHAPTER THIRTY-ONE

# *Together for Good*

s I sat in the third pew of a large church waiting for a Christmas program to start, my mind wandered. It had been almost a year since Kevin's illness, and we were all doing well. I reached over and squeezed Kevin's hand, he looked so healthy and happy. He was loving the new job that God had miraculously provided. Finally, he was at a place of balance. The play continued as I continued to recall our wilderness journey. At times, the sky was so dark and trees so tall, it seemed there would be no getting out in one piece. Other times, we saw evidence that the Shepherd was leading us and found great joy in that. Always, He was there but we would tend to forget when we didn't see.

In hindsight, there are so many things I wish I had done differently. I could have done them better. And yet that was not reason enough for God to stay away. He knew what my shortcomings would be and He loved me still. He knew if it were Him walking my path, He would have handled it with much more class. While His standard is high and His tolerance for sin extreme, He is so much more than that. He is love, He is patience and He is kindness. He is everything we are not and yet He still rejoices over us with singing. He cheers for us when we get it right, He aches for us when we are thinking wrong and He receives us back over and over again.

The trumpet blast nearly knocked me out of the pew. Suddenly this majestic-looking king and his entourage walked slowly toward the manger. It had never struck me quite like this before. Wealthy honored kings of some vast kingdoms journeyed to this poor stable to honor a newborn baby. The people in their kingdoms looked to them for direction and yet they came. Imagine the humility in the hearts of those three kings. God spoke to them and they listened.

How profound it must have been for Joseph and Mary to witness such a scene. How great Thou art—the Maker of heaven and earth, the Prince of peace, Mighty God, Holy One, my Father, my Friend, my Healer and my Master—all wrapped in little rags and resting in a stable surrounded by animals.

The world looked for the Messiah to come with pomp and circumstance. God's plan was far more brilliant. He came to a town that nobody cared about and allowed our Savior to be born in a barn. Over and over again, He demonstrates His power in the ordinary things of life. He uses the unlikely and humbles the proud. He is not impressed with our abilities, He created them. He is warmed, though, by our blind trust in a God we cannot see. He loves it when we trust His view instead of our own.

We celebrate this baby in the manger, not the fancy table settings or beautiful lights. We celebrate One who came to set us free from guilt and shame. He came to show, not just to tell us, who we are to Him.

Our Lord Jesus sat on a royal throne in a most holy place, free from all of the evils of this world. He saw our need and He stood up. He looked into His Father's eyes as He took off His beautiful robe. Feeling His heart beat in His chest, He stepped away from all that was safe into the ultimate of vulnerability.

He crawled into this tiny little wrapping and handed Himself over to us to do with as we would. He left peace and took on poverty. He left safety and surrounded Himself with sin. His emotions, His body, and His heart would be broken. He knew this, but He came to us anyway.

Jesus led us by example. He told us to walk the way He did. When He was accused He didn't become insecure, He remembered who He was. When He was mistreated He didn't fight back, He saw past it. When He should have turned his back on us all, He instead prayed, "Father forgive them, they don't know what they're doing."

In a day and age when our rights have become sacred, we must remember what Jesus did. He laid down His rights for the sake of His love for people. Imagine the change in our world if we had lines we wouldn't cross no matter what anyone else was doing. If we could remain kind even when others are cruel, what would happen?

This baby, whether we accept Him or not—has changed the world. I choose to celebrate Jesus this day and every day. Everything else pales in comparison. Lord Jesus, have mercy on us all! Give us eyes to see things the way You do. Give us a heart to love each other in the way You have loved us. Bring us to the place where our character matters more than our comfort. Fill us up with more of You. Thank You for Your kind and loving patience toward us. Thank You, Jesus, for bridging the gap between heaven and me so we could be together for good. I will forever be grateful for Your mercy in my wilderness. I love You. Amen.

*The end of the world is coming soon. Therefore, be earnest and disciplined in your prayers. Most important of all, continue to show deep love for each other, for love covers a multitude of sins* (1 Peter 4:7-8).

# Workshops and Retreats by Susie Larson

**The Gift of Balance**: Take time to look at the areas in life that pull us off course. We will talk about "physical life" (i.e. diet, exercise and time management) as well as "spiritual life" (i.e. spiritual diet, spiritual exercise and spiritual rest). You will receive practical tips to bring your physical life to a healthy balance and inspiration to have your spiritual life centered on the things that matter most.

**Beyond These Walls—the Journaling Experience:** Treat yourself to some time alone to reflect on your thoughts and prayers. Learn how to find your own way of recording your thoughts. You will be blessed when you see how healing journaling can be. (Workshop only.)

**Prayer that Changes Things:** A powerful workshop that explores Scripture to see what God requires of us. We will look at areas in our lives that may hinder our prayers. We will remember how much we are loved by God. We will learn of the power that we have access to because we belong to Him.

**The Incredible Power of Our Choices:** This, my most popular workshop, delves into our importance as human beings. We are so important that it matters deeply what we say, whom we walk with and what we do. We will look in detail at the ripples we are leaving. We will also look at the big picture so we can line ourselves up with God's plan for us.

**Finding God in the Wilderness:** Life is hard, but God is wonderfully good. We will spend time talking about the effects of long-term crisis and how to stay tender in the midst of it all. Issues such as waiting, hurting, forgiving and hoping are addressed. Join me for a time of healing and encouragement. (Workshop only.)

**God's Hidden Treasures:** In a world that tells us "you will be okay when …" it becomes hard to remember how important we are to Jesus. When our identity is settled in our hearts, we are affected in every way! Be encouraged to know that God does not just "tolerate" us, He loves us with an everlasting love. Know it and believe it!

**Simple Joy:** Making room for Jesus during the holidays. (Workshop only.)

## *Other Workshops Available …*

Holy Confidence, Humble Dependence

The Gift of Forgiveness

Faith that Moves Things

Our Powerful Words

*\* If necessary, a message will be designed
around a requested theme.*

## *For Booking Information:*

kmsmlarson@worldnet.att.net

# *About the Author*

 As a conference/retreat presenter, Susie Larson has spoken to thousands of women about such issues as prayer, balance and the power of our choices. Susie also works as a freelance writer for Focus on the Family's Growing Years Edition monthly magazine. She enjoys reading, writing, running and most of all, spending time with her family. Susie and her husband make their home in Andover, Minnesota, with their three precious sons.